# The Kabbalah of Meaning

—

**COURSE AUTHOR**
*Rabbi Naftali Silberberg*

**CURRICULUM DEVELOPMENT**
*Rabbi Lazer Gurkov*
*Rabbi Yochanan Rivkin*
*Rabbi Shmuel Super*

**INSTRUCTOR ADVISORY BOARD**
*Rabbi Yosef Levin*
*Rabbi Levi Greenberg*
*Rabbi Sender Geisinsky*
*Rabbi Yisrael Rice*
*Rabbi Zushe Rivkin*

Cover Art: *Speaking*
David Rakia, oil on canvas, Jerusalem

Printed in the United States of America

832 Eastern Parkway, Brooklyn, NY 11213



**718-221-6900**
**WWW.MYJLI.COM**

# The Kabbalah of Meaning

COURSE
TEXTBOOK

Jewish Wisdom for Finding the Purpose
That Connects All Parts of Life

The Rohr Jewish Learning Institute
gratefully acknowledges the pioneering
and ongoing support of

**George and Pamela Rohr**

Since its inception, the Rohr JLI has been
a beneficiary of the vision, generosity, care,
and concern of the Rohr family.

In the merit of the tens of thousands of hours
of Torah study by JLI students worldwide,
may they be blessed with health, *Yiddishe
nachas* from all their loved ones, and
extraordinary success in all their endeavors.

DEDICATED TO

## Eddie and Arlene Goldstein

With deep appreciation for their friendship, generosity, and enduring commitment to strengthening the future of the Jewish people.

Through the Goldstein Fellowship for JLI Teens, thousands of young Jews are gaining opportunities to explore their heritage, strengthen their Jewish identity, and emerge as leaders in their communities.

May they go from strength to strength, enjoying good health, happiness, and continued success in all their endeavors.

# Citation Types

**SCRIPTURE**

The icon for Scripture is based on the images of a scroll and a spiral. The scroll is a literal reference; the spiral symbolizes Scripture's role as the singular source from which all subsequent Torah knowledge emanates.

**SCRIPTURAL COMMENTARY**

Throughout the ages, Jews have scrutinized the Torah's text, generating many commentaries.

**TALMUD AND MIDRASH**

The Talmud and Midrash record the teachings of the sages—fundamental links in the unbroken chain of the Torah's transmission going back to Mount Sinai.

**TALMUDIC COMMENTARY**

The layers of Talmudic teaching have been rigorously excavated in each era, resulting in a library of insightful commentaries.

**JEWISH MYSTICISM**

The mystics explore the inner, esoteric depths. The icon for mystical texts reflects the "*sefirot* tree" commonly present in kabbalistic charts.

**CHARACTER AND VIRTUE**

Often called *musar*, this literature provides character refinement and personal development strategies.

**JEWISH PHILOSOPHY**

Jewish philosophic texts shed light on life's big questions and demonstrate the relevance of Jewish teachings even as the sands of societal values continuously shift.

**JEWISH LAW AND CUSTOM**

The guidance that emerges from Scripture and the Talmud finds practical expression in Jewish law, known as *Halachah* ("the way"), alongside customs adopted by Jewish communities through the generations.

***CHASIDUT***

Chasidism's advent in the eighteenth century brought major, encouraging changes to Jewish life and outlook. Its teachings are akin to refreshing, life-sustaining waters from a continuously flowing well of the profoundest insights.

**LITURGY**

The texts of the Jewish prayer book burst with the full spectrum of human emotion: from joy, to longing, to contrition, and to hope. They all share the authentic search for a meaningful encounter with G-d.

**PERSPECTIVES**

Personal, professional, and academic perspectives, expressed in essays, research papers, diaries, and other works, can often enhance appreciation for Torah ideas and the totality of the Jewish experience.

# Contents

IN TRIBUTE TO

**Rabbi Moshe Kotlarsky**

of blessed memory

**הרב החסיד ר' משה יהודא ב"ר צבי יוסף ע"ה**

Our longstanding visionary chairman, entrusted and empowered by the Rebbe to facilitate the growth and expansion of the network of Chabad *shluchim* and its institutions worldwide.

יהא זכרו ברוך

## Foreword

THE END OF THE MATTER, AFTER EVERYTHING IS CONSIDERED: REVERE G-D AND KEEP HIS COMMANDMENTS—BECAUSE THAT'S WHAT IT MEANS TO BE HUMAN.

—ECCLESIASTES 12:13

From the moment we're old enough to ask "Why?" we begin our search for meaning. We want to know that our lives matter, that our struggles count for something, and that the people we love and the things we do are not arbitrary or fleeting. Yet, in a world that moves quickly and rewards productivity over purpose, these questions often go unanswered.

Judaism has never asked us to choose between belief and meaning, or between purpose and reality. Instead, it offers a framework in which every part of life—sacred or mundane, joyful or painful—can be filled with purpose.

*The Kabbalah of Meaning*, the latest offering of the Rohr Jewish Learning Institute, explores that framework. Drawing on a rich range of Jewish texts, from Torah and Talmud to Chasidic thought, it offers six fresh lenses through which to view our personal journeys. What does it mean to have a mission in life? How do we make sense of the events that unfold around us? Can daily life—routine, repetitive, and often unremarkable—become a vessel for something larger? And what is our essential identity beneath all our roles and labels?

Each lesson addresses a different facet of human experience: from our need for agency, to the meaning of time, to the value of the unchosen. Rather than offering quick fixes, this course invites real reflection, grounded in ancient wisdom and relevant to today's inner lives.

We hope that *The Kabbalah of Meaning* will not only answer questions you've asked, but give you new tools—and perhaps a new vocabulary—for asking deeper ones. Most of all, we hope it will help each of us live with more clarity, connection, and meaning.

## Continuing Education Credits

### FOR MEDICAL PRACTITIONERS

#### ACCREDITATION STATEMENT

This activity has been planned and implemented in accordance with the accreditation requirements and policies of the **Accreditation Council for Continuing Medical Education (ACCME)** through the joint providership of New York Medical College and the Rohr Jewish Learning Institute. New York Medical College is accredited by the ACCME to provide continuing medical education for physicians.

#### CREDITS DESIGNATION

New York Medical College designates this live activity for a maximum of ***9.0 AMA PRA Category I Credits™***. Physicians should claim only the credit commensurate with the extent of their participation in the activity.

#### AMERICANS WITH DISABILITIES ACT STATEMENT

New York Medical College fully complies with the legal requirements of the Americans with Disabilities Act. If you require special assistance, please submit your request in writing, thirty (30) days in advance of the activity, to continuingeducation@myjli.com

#### CONFLICT OF INTEREST DISCLOSURE POLICY

The **Conflict of Interest Disclosure Policy** of New York Medical College requires that faculty participating in any CME activity disclose to the audience any relationship(s) with a pharmaceutical product or device company. Any presenter whose disclosed relationships prove to create a conflict of interest, with regard to their contribution to the activity, will not be permitted to present.

New York Medical College also requires that faculty participating in any CME activity disclose to the audience when discussing any unlabeled or investigational use of any commercial product or device not yet approved for use in the United States. New York Medical College and ACCME staff have no conflicts of interest with commercial interests related directly or indirectly to this educational activity.

#### DISCLOSURE OF COMMERCIAL SUPPORT AND THE UNLABELED USE OF A COMMERCIAL PRODUCT

No member of the planning committee and no member of the faculty for this event has a financial interest or other relationship with any commercial product.

The members of the Planning Committee are:

**Edward I. Reichman, M.D.**—*Reviewer*
*Professor of Emergency Medicine and Epidemiology and Population Health,*
*Albert Einstein College of Medicine*

**Mindy Wallach**—*Course Administrator*
*The Rohr Jewish Learning Institute/The Wellness Institute*

Disclosure: The members of the Planning Committee present no relevant conflict of interest.

**To obtain credit** for attending the course (9 credits max.): Medical doctors should complete the registration form at **www.myjli.com/cme at the beginning of the course**. Mental health professionals should inform their instructor that they are seeking credit and provide them with their full professional name, professional credentials, and state(s) they are licensed to practice in.

# Continuing Education Credits

## FOR PSYCHOLOGISTS AND MENTAL HEALTH PROFESSIONALS

### ACCREDITATION STATEMENT

The Wellness Institute is approved by the **American Psychological Association** to sponsor continuing education for psychologists. The Wellness Institute maintains responsibility for this program and its content.

**CREDITS PER SESSION:** 1.5

### BEHAVIORAL LESSON OBJECTIVES FOR PSYCHOLOGISTS

**LESSON 1**

1. Explain the importance of meaningfulness to experiencing happiness and well-being.
2. Discuss key meaning-makers, including: personal growth, productivity, and genuine relationships.

**LESSON 2**

1. Explain hedonic adaptation and the futility of material pursuits as a reliable source of happiness and well-being.
2. Discuss the benefits of altruism and how contributing to the community and world provides purpose.

**LESSON 3**

1. Explain the relationship between purpose (goals) and meaningfulness.
2. Discuss how an overarching purpose in life can infuse all tasks, big and mundane, with meaning.

**LESSON 4**

1. Discuss how meaningfulness can be found in each stage of life and the present juncture in time.
2. Examine the importance of time and finding meaning by celebrating milestones, holidays, and birthdays.

**LESSON 5**

1. Explain how faith provides meaning and hope, even in times of disappointment or challenge.
2. Discuss the lessons and purpose that can be gleaned from disappointing turns in life.

**LESSON 6**

1. Explain mattering and the correlations between self-worth and well-being.
2. Discuss perspectives on the inherent self-worth of every individual to access in times of self-doubt.

**The Wellness Institute** is recognized by the **New York State** Education Department's State Board for Psychology as an approved provider of continuing education for **Licensed Psychologists** #PSY-0220; by the New York State Education Department's State Board for Social Work as an approved provider of continuing education for **Licensed Master Social Workers (LMSWs)** and **Licensed Clinical Social Workers (LCSWs)** #SW-0741; by the New York State Education Department's State Board for Mental Health Practitioners as an approved provider of continuing education for **Licensed Mental Health Counselors (LMHCs)** #MHC-0270 and **Licensed Marriage and Family Therapists (LMFTs)** #MFT-0114 in New York.

---

Psychologists, Social Workers, LMFTs, and LPC/LMHCs in many states can satisfy their CE requirements by participating in this course. To verify if your profession is covered, inquire via email: continuingeducation@myjli.com. Include your name, credentials, and state(s) you are licensed to practice in.

## Endorsements

The JLI Meaning Course is a timely and deeply relevant initiative. It brings Viktor Frankl's legacy into the present with clarity, integrity, and heart. In a world increasingly in search of purpose, this course offers not only insight, but orientation.

**PROFESSOR ALEXANDER BATTHYÁNY, PhD**

Director, Viktor Frankl Institute, Vienna

Director, Research Institute for Theoretical Psychology and Personalist Studies, Pázmány University, Budapest

---

Why are we here? What does it all mean? The technological marvels and material abundance of modern life leave many people paradoxically groping for answers to these eternal questions. Ancient wisdom, spiritual striving, and modern psychological research all have something to offer. The questions are eternal; the answers are diverse and variable. This course promises to equip people to grapple more effectively with life's mysteries.

**ROY F. BAUMEISTER, PhD**

President,
International Positive Psychology Association

Emeritus Professor,
University of Queensland School of Psychology

Author, *Meanings of Life*,
*The Self Explained*, and other titles

---

If you are in search of greater meaning and purpose in your own life, take this course on *The Kabbalah of Meaning*! It bridges the centuries-old wisdom of Kabbalah with modern psychological knowledge to create a guide for fostering a life worth living. Participants will leave inspired.

**KENNETH I. PARGAMENT, PhD**

Professor Emeritus, Department of Psychology Bowling Green State University

Co-Editor, APA Handbook of Psychology, Religion, and Spirituality

Author, *Working with Spiritual Struggles in Psychotherapy*, and other titles

---

Thank you for bringing this intriguing course to my attention. Throughout the lifespan, meaning can be found in events large and small; religion and spirituality form a vital resource that facilitates meaning-making in good times as well as in challenging times. In six lessons, this course blends core life pursuits—meaning, spirituality, and connection—and shows how they offer more fulfillment than materialism, leading to a richer, more fulfilling life.

**MICHAEL E. NIELSEN, PhD**

Professor, Department of Psychology
Georgia Southern University

It's refreshing to see a course that deals with how to do life right from the start: not just putting out the fires and navigating the storms, but the basic details of why you are here, what you need to get done, and how to do it right. That' s called healthy, wholesome living. That's exactly what *The Kabbalah of Meaning* is all about.

**RABBI TZVI FREEMAN**

Senior Editor, Chabad.org

Author, *Bringing Heaven Down to Earth*, and other titles

---

Science shows us that we all are built with an innate "neural docking station" for a sacred transcendent awareness. We are inherently born to see relational spirituality with Hashem and His magnificent presence in our love for fellow human beings and living beings. However, this gift is one-third innate and two-thirds environmentally formed, which means we must always continue to learn, to foster our own birthright of spiritual awareness. Foremost we must prepare ourselves to serve as spiritual ambassadors of our children, to embrace their natural core for spiritual formation.

**LISA MILLER, PhD**

Professor of Psychology

Founder, the Spirituality Mind Body Institute, Columbia University

Author, *The Awakened Brain: The New Science of Spirituality and Our Quest for an Inspired Life*, and other titles

---

The pace of society today exceeds many people's capacity to adapt enough to achieve their ideals. It's easy to be distracted, anxious, or confused about how to set and reach major life goals. Even the expectations we strive to live by can be easily misunderstood, miscommunicated, or, at times, counterproductive. It takes more than sheer will power to find spiritual balance and meaning in today's world. The Rohr JLI's new course, *The Kabbalah of Meaning*, provides science-based tools and lessons for people to grow purpose and intentional communities with each other. This is a valuable course that would benefit everyone. Such a resource is sorely needed for people to create the "good life" today, and society needs us at our best more than ever.

**GIACOMO BONO, PhD**

Professor of Psychology
California State University, Dominguez Hills

Co-Author, *Making Grateful Kids: The Science of Building Character*

Experiencing meaning in life, living with purpose, and feeling happy and fulfilled have arguably always been primary motivations for human beings. These issues feel especially urgent today, given how many aspects of modern society—such as social media addiction, the threats posed by artificial intelligence, political polarization, war, and general widespread distrust of each other—threaten to undermine our sense of meaning and connection. A course focused specifically on these concerns is not only timely but incredibly necessary. I applaud the Rohr Jewish Learning Institute for offering such a course, dedicated to enhancing the well-being of its students and, by extension, contributing to a healthier world.

**JOSHUA HICKS, PhD**

Professor, Department of
Psychological and Brain Sciences
Texas A&M University

Co-Editor, *The Experience of Meaning in Life*

---

In these turbulent times, when moral and societal challenges feel overwhelming, I believe this course can offer a meaningful anchor. It's designed to help individuals reconnect with their spiritual lives and find grounding amid uncertainty. The search for meaning is something I've found to be a lifelong journey, and through a Jewish perspective, participants may discover a clearer sense of purpose, deeper inner peace, and a renewed connection to the greater whole of our society. My hope is that this experience will not only enrich your personal path but also strengthen the bonds that tie us together as a community.

**GINA M. BRELSFORD, PhD**

Professor of Psychology
Director, Honors programs
Penn State Harrisburg

---

Why am I here? What is my purpose in life? What is the point of the tedious, annoying, and downright difficult tasks demanded of me to keep things going? They seem unrelated to my yearnings and ambitions. We can try to figure it out on our own, or we can delve into ancient texts that contain the time-tested wisdom of scholars and mystics who recorded their insights for posterity. Or else we can do it the JLI way, which is to employ both methods: to study the source texts, and discuss and debate what they mean for us in the here and now. This latest course from JLI, *The Kabbalah of Meaning*, accomplishes this with the professionalism and appeal that the many participants of past courses have come to expect and appreciate.

**RABBI YANKI TAUBER**

Editor, *The Book of Jewish Knowledge*

Author, *The Book of Genesis: With Commentary and Insights from 500 Sages and Mystics*, *Inside Time*, and other titles on Jewish mysticism

LESSON 1

## THE MEANING WE SEEK

*When we have it all, we still need something more: purpose. Discover four fundamental human qualities that provide lasting fulfillment.*

**A CYNICAL MOSAIC (AS IN ECCLESIASTES) (DETAIL)**
Berit Engen, woven tapestry, linen yarn, Oak Park, Illinois, 2013

## I. THE DEPTHS OF FUTILITY

Welcome to *The Kabbalah of Meaning*!

We are blessed by G-d* and live in an era of abundance. Never before have so many people had access to wealth, health, education, and personal freedom. Yet, despite—or perhaps because of—this unprecedented prosperity, many feel an acute sense of emptiness. We check off the boxes: financial stability, physical well-being, literacy and knowledge, even strong relationships—yet, for many, something remains elusive. As opposed to other quantifiable goals and aspirations we have, this one is more intangible.

*Throughout this book, "G-d" and "L-rd" are written with a hyphen instead of an "o" (both in our own translations and when quoting others). This is one way we accord reverence to the sacred Divine name. This also reminds us that, even as we seek G-d, He transcends any human effort to describe His reality.

In this course, we will look to the Torah for answers to the all-important question: What does it mean to live a meaningful life? As we will discover in today's lesson and the ones that follow, there are multiple layers to the answer.

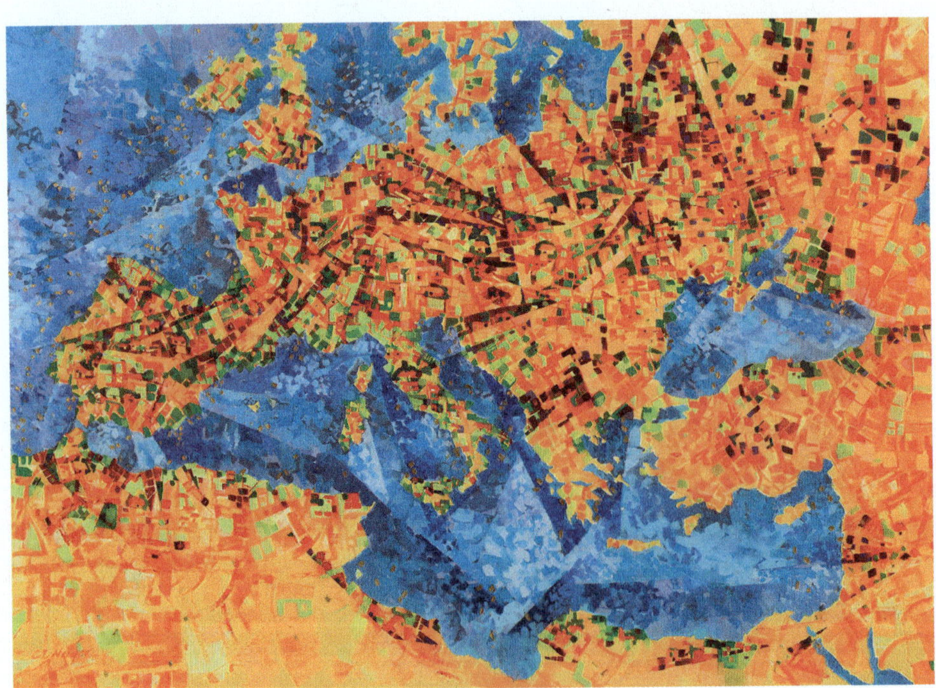

**WISDOM'S WANDERING**
Carol Neiger, oil and gold leaf on canvas, Permanent Collection, Hillel at Northwestern University

**TEXT 1**

## “All Is Futile”

Ecclesiastes 1:1–4

דִּבְרֵי קֹהֶלֶת בֶּן דָּוִד מֶלֶךְ בִּירוּשָׁלָם:

הֲבֵל הֲבָלִים אָמַר קֹהֶלֶת, הֲבֵל הֲבָלִים הַכֹּל הָבֶל.

מַה יִּתְרוֹן לָאָדָם בְּכָל עֲמָלוֹ שֶׁיַּעֲמֹל תַּחַת הַשָּׁמֶשׁ?

דּוֹר הֹלֵךְ וְדוֹר בָּא, וְהָאָרֶץ לְעוֹלָם עֹמָדֶת.

The words of Kohelet, son of
David, king in Jerusalem:

Futility of futilities, said Kohelet;
futility of futilities, all is futile.

What profit has man in all his toil
that he toils under the sun?

A generation goes and a generation comes,
but [only] the earth endures forever.

#### ECCLESIASTES

Biblical book. Written by King Solomon, Ecclesiastes is part of the Writings section of the Tanach. Addressing the existential question of the meaning of life, Ecclesiastes exposes the futility of materialism, concluding that Divine worship and *mitzvah* observance are the only true meaning of life. This book is traditionally read in many communities during the holiday of Sukkot.

**TEXT 2**

## Mental Health Crisis

Lisa Miller, *The Awakened Brain: The New Science of Spirituality and Our Quest for an Inspired Life* (New York: Random House, 2021), p. 4

Depression, anxiety, and substance abuse have reached epidemic proportions globally. In 2017, 66.6 million Americans—more than half of the

#### LISA MILLER, PHD

Psychologist and author. Lisa Miller serves as a professor of psychology and education at Teachers College, Columbia University, and is the founder of their Spirituality Mind Body Institute, a graduate program in spirituality and psychology. Her research focuses on the quantifiable effects of spirituality in mental health, and she is the author of *The Spiritual Child* and *The Awakened Brain*.

respondents on the National Survey on Drug Use and Health—reported binge drinking within the past month, and 20 million met the criteria for a substance use disorder. Thirty-one percent of American adults will develop a full-blown anxiety disorder at some point in their lives, and 19 percent in any given year. The World Health Organization reports that 264 million people on the planet are depressed; depression is the third most costly disability worldwide. Each year, 17 million American adults are depressed. Over 16 percent of youth in late adolescence currently face depression, and the impact of depression on suicide accounts for *the second leading cause of death* in adolescents, rivaled only by death by auto accident....

While the stakes of our mental health crisis are truly life and death, many of us also suffer from less debilitating, though still painful, conditions: burnout and chronic stress; trouble concentrating and connecting; loneliness and isolation; lives that are rich in many ways yet feel somehow narrow, hollow, and cut off. Even when we experience success and satisfaction, we may sense that there's more to happiness—that life could be more joyful, rewarding, and meaningful.

## II. SELF-ALIGNMENT

Solving the crisis of meaning requires us to turn inside and define who we actually are.

**SELF-PORTRAIT**
Leonid Balaklav, oil on canvas, Israel, 1997

**EXERCISE 1.1**

**Describe at least one activity that brings you pleasure *and* that you find meaningful.**

**Describe at least one activity that brings you pleasure but which you do not find meaningful.**

**Describe at least one activity that you find meaningful but which does not bring you pleasure.**

**TEXT 3**

## Preserving Trees

Deuteronomy 20:19

כִּי תָצוּר אֶל עִיר יָמִים רַבִּים לְהִלָּחֵם עָלֶיהָ לְתָפְשָׂהּ, לֹא
תַשְׁחִית אֶת עֵצָהּ לִנְדֹּחַ עָלָיו גַּרְזֶן, כִּי מִמֶּנּוּ תֹאכֵל וְאֹתוֹ
לֹא תִכְרֹת, כִּי הָאָדָם עֵץ הַשָּׂדֶה לָבֹא מִפָּנֶיךָ בַּמָּצוֹר.

When you besiege a city for many days, waging war against it to capture it, do not destroy its trees by wielding an axe against them, for from them you shall eat, and you shall not cut them down. For the tree of the field is a human, that you should besiege it?

**EXERCISE 1.2**

**With a partner, come up with as many similarities as possible between trees and humans.**

1.

2.

3.

4.

5.

FIGURE 1.1

## Key Tree Characteristics

1. Personal Growth
2. Productivity
3. Giving
4. Relationships

Sarah Kranz, 2000

## III. PERSONAL GROWTH

The Torah compares humans to trees, so for clues to our fundamental characteristics we will examine the qualities of trees, and we'll explore how these qualities play out in our human lives. Our first quality is growth.

**A PAIR OF BREEDS**
Menucha Yankelevitch,
oil on canvas, Israel, 2007

**TEXT 4**

## Humans and Trees

Talmud, Taanit 7a

מַאי דִכְתִיב: "כִּי הָאָדָם עֵץ הַשָּׂדֶה", וְכִי אָדָם עֵץ שָׂדֶה הוּא?

אֶלָא, מִשּׁוּם דִכְתִיב: "כִּי מִמֶנוּ תֹאכֵל וְאֹתוֹ לֹא תִכְרֹת", וּכְתִיב: "אֹתוֹ תַשְׁחִית וְכָרָתָּ".

הָא כֵּיצַד?

אִם תַּלְמִיד חָכָם הָגוּן הוּא – "מִמֶנוּ תֹאכֵל וְאֹתוֹ לֹא תִכְרֹת", וְאִם לָאו – "אֹתוֹ תַשְׁחִית וְכָרָתָּ".

What is the meaning of the verse: "For the tree of the field is a human"? Is man actually a tree of the field?

Earlier in the same verse it is written, "For from them you shall eat, and you shall not cut them down," and it is written in the next verse, "[However, if it is a tree that you know is not a food tree] you may destroy and cut it down."

[This indicates that there are certain trees that may be cut down, while others may not be destroyed.] How so?

If a Torah scholar is worthy: "From them you shall eat, and you shall not cut them down," but if he is not worthy: "He you may destroy and cut down."

**BABYLONIAN TALMUD**

A literary work of monumental proportions that draws upon the legal, spiritual, intellectual, ethical, and historical traditions of Judaism. The 37 tractates of the Babylonian Talmud contain the teachings of the Jewish sages from the period after the destruction of the 2nd Temple through the 5th century CE. It has served as the primary vehicle for the transmission of the Oral Law and the education of Jews over the centuries; it is the entry point for all subsequent legal, ethical, and theological Jewish scholarship.

**TEXT 5**

## Ascending Spirit

Ecclesiastes 3:21

מִי יוֹדֵעַ רוּחַ בְּנֵי הָאָדָם הָעֹלָה הִיא לְמָעְלָה,
וְרוּחַ הַבְּהֵמָה הַיֹּרֶדֶת הִיא לְמַטָּה לָאָרֶץ.

How many understand that the spirit of the human ascends on high, while the spirit of the beast descends to the earth?

**FIGURE 1.2**

## *Mensch* Definition

**mensch** noun

*/ men(t)sh /*

: a person of integrity and honor

**menschy (men(t)-she)** adjective

TEXT 6

## *Mensch* or Human?

Rabbi Mendy Herson, "On Being a Mentsch," Chabad.org

What is the Torah definition of a human? A human has the capacity for self-assessment. A human has the mental and moral capacity to override impulse (can a dog decide to go on a diet?). A human can choose to follow his moral compass instead of his physical inclination. A human can calculate consequences beyond the immediate. That is the Torah description of a human, the Torah definition of a *mentsch* . . . something we should all strive for.

Interestingly, the term has different connotations when used in American parlance. When a person is weak and less than noble, impulse-driven instead of morally focused, what do we say?

"Listen, he's only human!"

In our vernacular, recognizing that a person is "human" is acknowledging his inherent weakness. We see a human as inherently flawed and morally feeble. We cut a guy slack because we know he can't reach a noble goal; after all, he's only human! What can you really expect from this person of flesh and blood?

Think about it. The Torah/Jewish term of human—*mentsch*—is something to strive for, while the American "human" is a fallback position in case of moral failure.

**RABBI MENDY HERSON**

A native of New Jersey, Rabbi Mendy Herson received his rabbinic ordination from the Central Lubavitcher Yeshiva in Brooklyn, NY. He serves as the Director of Chabad of New Jersey and as the Dean of the Rabbinical College of America in Morristown, New Jersey.

**EXERCISE 1.3**

**In which ways have you grown and improved as a human being?**

**Which areas can use improvement?**

**What are ways to implement that in your life?**

## IV. PRODUCTIVITY

Now for the next obvious thing about trees: in addition to growing, they produce, and their fruits benefit the world.

**FRUIT OF HER LABOR**
Yoram Lukov (b. 1940), oil on canvas, Israel

**TEXT 7**

## Fruitful Trees

The Rebbe, Rabbi Menachem Mendel Schneerson,
*Torat Menachem* 5744:2, p. 904

עִנְיָנוֹ שֶׁל "אִילָן" הוּא - "עֵץ .. עוֹשֶׂה פְּרִי" (בְּרֵאשִׁית א, יא), הַיְינוּ, **עֵץ** שֶׁעוֹשֶׂה **פֵּירוֹת**, וּבְאוֹפֶן שֶׁ"זַרְעוֹ בוֹ" - "גַרְעִינֵי כָּל פְּרִי שֶׁמֵהֶן הָאִילָן צוֹמֵחַ כְּשֶׁנּוֹטְעִין אוֹתָן" (רַשִׁ"י עַל הַפָּסוּק) . . .

וְעִנְיָן זֶה מוּדְגָשׁ בְּיוֹתֵר בְּ"רֹאשׁ הַשָּׁנָה לָאִילָן" - שֶׁהֲרֵי כָּל הָעִנְיָן דְ"רֹאשׁ הַשָּׁנָה לָאִילָן" **בַּהֲלָכָה** אֵינוֹ אֶלָּא בְּקֶשֶׁר **לְפֵירוֹת** הָאִילָן, "שֶׁאֵין מְעַשְׂרִין **פֵּירוֹת** הָאִילָן שֶׁחָנְטוּ קוֹדֶם שְׁבָט עַל שֶׁחָנְטוּ לְאַחַר שְׁבָט" (רַשִׁ"י רֵישׁ רֹאשׁ הַשָּׁנָה).

A tree, by definition, is meant to produce fruit—like the verse says, "a tree that produces fruit" (GENESIS 1:11). That means it grows fruit in a way where "its seed is within it" (IBID.), meaning that each fruit contains seeds that can grow into another tree (RASHI, AD LOC.). . . .

This idea is underscored by the New Year for Trees on the fifteenth of Shevat because the Halachic importance of this day is all about the tree's *fruits*. As Rashi explains (ROSH HASHANAH 2A), we don't combine fruits that ripened before Shevat with those that ripened after when calculating tithes.

**RABBI MENACHEM MENDEL SCHNEERSON 1902–1994**

The towering Jewish leader of the 20th century, known as "the Lubavitcher Rebbe," or simply as "the Rebbe." Born in southern Ukraine, the Rebbe escaped Nazi-occupied Europe, arriving in the U.S. in June 1941. The Rebbe inspired and guided the revival of traditional Judaism after the European devastation, impacting virtually every Jewish community the world over. The Rebbe often emphasized that the performance of just one additional good deed could usher in the era of Mashiach. The Rebbe's scholarly talks and writings have been printed in more than 200 volumes.

**TEXT 8**

## Leaving Directions

Jerusalem Talmud, Orlah 1:3

כֵּיצַד הוּא יוֹדֵעַ?

רִבִּי בִּיבַי בְּשֵׁם רִבִּי חֲנִינָה: אִם הָיוּ הֶעָלִים הֲפוּכִין כְּלַפֵּי הַיַלְדָה דָבָר בָּרִיא שֶׁהוּא חַי מִכֹּחַ הַזְקֵנָה, וְאִם הָיוּ הֶעָלִים הֲפוּכִין כְּלַפֵּי הַזְקֵנָה דָבָר בָּרִיא שֶׁהוּא חַי מִכֹּחַ הַיַלְדָה.

אָמַר רִבִּי יוּדָן בַּר חָנִין: סִימָנָא - דְאָכִל מִן חַבְרֵיהּ בְּהִית מִסְתַּכְּלָא בֵיהּ.

How can one determine [whether the young tree is self-reliant]?

Rabbi Bibi said in the name of Rabbi Chaninah: If the leaves of the young tree are turned inward, toward itself, one may be sure that it lives from the old one. If the leaves are turned toward the old tree, one may be sure that the young one is self-sustaining.

Rabbi Yudan bar Chanin said: Here is a sign: one who eats from their friend is ashamed to look at them.

**JERUSALEM TALMUD**

A commentary to the Mishnah compiled during the 4th and 5th centuries. The Jerusalem Talmud predates its Babylonian counterpart by 100 years and is written in both Hebrew and Aramaic. While the Babylonian Talmud is the most authoritative source for Jewish law, the Jerusalem Talmud remains an invaluable source for the spiritual, intellectual, ethical, historical, and legal traditions of Judaism.

**TEXT 9**

## Producing Our Own

Talmud, Bava Metzi'a 38a

אָדָם רוֹצֶה בְּקַב שֶׁלוֹ מִתִּשְׁעָה קַבִּים שֶׁל חֲבֵירוֹ.

A person prefers one measure of their own over nine measures of their friend's.

**EXERCISE 1.4**

**In which ways have you been or are you currently productive?**

**In which areas can you be more productive?**

**What are some ways to implement these in your life?**

## V. HELPING OTHERS

The next piece of self-awareness and self-knowledge that we can learn from trees is the act of benefiting others.

**TWO BOYS**
Zvi Malnovitzer
(b. 1945), Israel, 2006

**TEXT 10**

## Offspring Like You

Talmud, Taanit 5b–6a

כִּי הֲווֹ מִיפַּטְרִי מֵהֲדָדֵי, אֲמַר לֵיהּ: לִיבָרְכָן מַר!

אֲמַר לֵיהּ: אֶמְשׁוֹל לְךָ מָשָׁל, לְמָה הַדָּבָר דּוֹמֶה? לְאָדָם שֶׁהָיָה הוֹלֵךְ בַּמִּדְבָּר וְהָיָה רָעֵב וְעָיֵף וְצָמֵא, וּמָצָא אִילָן שֶׁפֵּירוֹתָיו מְתוּקִין וְצִלּוֹ נָאֶה וְאַמַּת הַמַּיִם עוֹבֶרֶת תַּחְתָּיו. אָכַל מִפֵּירוֹתָיו, וְשָׁתָה מִמֵּימָיו, וְיָשַׁב בְּצִילּוֹ.

וּכְשֶׁבִּיקֵּשׁ לֵילֵךְ, אָמַר: אִילָן אִילָן, בַּמָּה אֲבָרֶכְךָ? אִם אוֹמַר לְךָ שֶׁיְּהוּ פֵּירוֹתֶיךָ מְתוּקִין – הֲרֵי פֵּירוֹתֶיךָ מְתוּקִין, שֶׁיְּהֵא צִילְּךָ נָאֶה – הֲרֵי צִילְּךָ נָאֶה, שֶׁתְּהֵא אַמַּת הַמַּיִם עוֹבֶרֶת תַּחְתֶּיךָ – הֲרֵי אַמַּת הַמַּיִם עוֹבֶרֶת תַּחְתֶּיךָ, אֶלָּא: יְהִי רָצוֹן שֶׁכָּל נְטִיעוֹת שֶׁנּוֹטְעִין מִמְּךָ יִהְיוּ כְּמוֹתְךָ.

אַף אַתָּה, בַּמָּה אֲבָרֶכְךָ? אִם בְּתוֹרָה – הֲרֵי תּוֹרָה, אִם בְּעוֹשֶׁר – הֲרֵי עוֹשֶׁר, אִם בְּבָנִים – הֲרֵי בָּנִים, אֶלָּא: יְהִי רָצוֹן שֶׁיִּהְיוּ צֶאֱצָאֵי מֵעֶיךָ כְּמוֹתְךָ.

When they were taking leave of one another, Rabbi Nachman said to Rabbi Yitzchak: "Master, give me a blessing."

Rabbi Yitzchak said to him: "I will tell you a parable. This situation is comparable to one who was walking through a desert and who was hungry, tired, and thirsty. He found a tree whose fruits were sweet and whose shade was pleasant, and a stream of water flowed beneath it. He ate from the fruits of the tree, drank from the water in the stream, and sat in the shade of the tree.

"When he wished to leave, he said: 'Tree, tree, with what shall I bless you? If I say to you that your fruits should be sweet, your fruits are already sweet. If I say that your shade should be pleasant, your shade is already pleasant. If I say that a stream of water should flow beneath you, a stream of water already flows beneath you. Rather, I will bless you as follows: May it be G-d's will that all saplings that they plant from you be like you.'

"So it is with you. With what shall I bless you? If I bless you with Torah, you already have Torah. If I bless you with wealth, you already have wealth. If I bless you with children, you already have children. Rather, may it be G-d's will that your offspring shall be like you."

**TEXT 11**

## "Existential Mattering"

Joshua A. Hicks and Laura A. King, "Three Ways to See Meaning in Your Life," *Greater Good Magazine: Science-Based Insights for a Meaningful Life*, November, 2021

There is great comfort in believing that your life and actions matter in the grand scheme of things. This conviction is referred to as "existential mattering" and is a strong component of the experience of meaning in life. While the concept of existential mattering often evokes images of famous (and infamous) people who have done extraordinary things in their lives . . . many people gain a sense of mattering through avenues more easily traversed.

Research shows that feeling that you have made a positive influence on others is, unsurprisingly, almost always associated with the belief that your life is meaningful. Existential mattering then is often rooted in the sense that you matter to *others*—from helping strangers in need and providing social support to loved ones, to simply being a reliable friend.

**JOSHUA A. HICKS, PHD**

Psychology professor. Joshua Hicks received his PhD in personality and social psychology from the University of Missouri, and he currently serves as a professor in the department of psychological and brain sciences at Texas A&M University. His research focuses on the experience of meaning in life, and authenticity.

**LAURA A. KING, PHD**

Psychology professor. Laura King received her PhD in personality psychology from the University of California, Davis, and she currently serves as a professor of psychological sciences at the University of Missouri, Columbia. Her research focuses on the experience of meaning in life, and morality.

TEXT 12

## Need to Give

Talmud, Pesachim 112a

אָמַר לוֹ: "בְּנִי, יוֹתֵר מִמַּה שֶׁהָעֵגֶל רוֹצֶה
לִינַק, פָּרָה רוֹצָה לְהָנִיק".

Rabbi Akiva responded, "My son, more than the calf desires to nurse, the cow wants to give milk."

TEXT 13

## Inequitable Kindness

Midrash, *Tanchuma*, Mishpatim 9

אָמַר דָוִד לִפְנֵי הַקָדוֹשׁ בָּרוּךְ הוּא, "רִבּוֹן הָעוֹלָם . . .
תְּיַישֵׁר עוֹלָמְךָ בְּשָׁוֶה, הָעֲשִׁירִים וְהָעֲנִיִּים!"

אָמַר לוֹ, "אִם כֵּן, 'חֶסֶד וֶאֱמֶת מַן יִנְצְרוּהוּ?' (תְּהִלִּים סא, ח).
אִם יִהְיוּ כֻּלָּם עֲשִׁירִים אוֹ עֲנִיִּים, מִי יוּכַל לַעֲשׂוֹת חֶסֶד?"

King David said to G-d, "Master of the universe! . . . Establish equity in Your world by making rich and poor the same!"

G-d replied, "If such were the case, 'Who would preserve kindness and truth?' (PSALMS 61:8) If all were rich or all were poor, who would be able to do acts of kindness?"

***TANCHUMA***

A Midrashic work bearing the name of Rabbi Tanchuma, a 4th-century Talmudic sage quoted often in this work. "Midrash" is the designation of a particular genre of rabbinic literature usually forming a running commentary on specific books of the Bible. *Tanchuma* provides textual exegeses, expounds upon the biblical narrative, and develops and illustrates moral principles. *Tanchuma* is unique in that many of its sections commence with a Halachic discussion, which subsequently leads into non-Halachic teachings.

**TEXT 14**

## Poor Charity

Rabbi Yosef Caro, Shulchan Aruch, *Yoreh De'ah* 248:1

כָּל אָדָם חַיָּיב לִיתֵּן צְדָקָה. אֲפִילוּ עָנִי הַמִּתְפַּרְנֵס מִן הַצְּדָקָה חַיָּיב לִיתֵּן מִמָּה שֶׁיִּתְּנוּ לוֹ.

Everyone is obligated to give charity. Even a poor person who relies on charitable support themselves must give from what they receive.

**RABBI YOSEF CARO (MARAN, *BEIT YOSEF*) 1488–1575**

Halachic authority and author. Rabbi Caro was born in Spain but was forced to flee during the Expulsion in 1492 and eventually settled in Safed, Israel. He authored many works, including the *Beit Yosef*, *Kesef Mishneh*, and a mystical work, *Magid Meisharim*. Rabbi Caro's magnum opus, the Shulchan Aruch (Code of Jewish Law), has been universally accepted as the basis for modern Jewish law.

**EXERCISE 1.5**

**In which ways have you been or are you currently helping others—spiritually, emotionally, or financially?**

**In which areas can you increase in your giving?**

**What are some ways to implement that in your life?**

## VI. GENUINE RELATIONSHIPS

Our final category of core human qualities is our capacity for relationships.

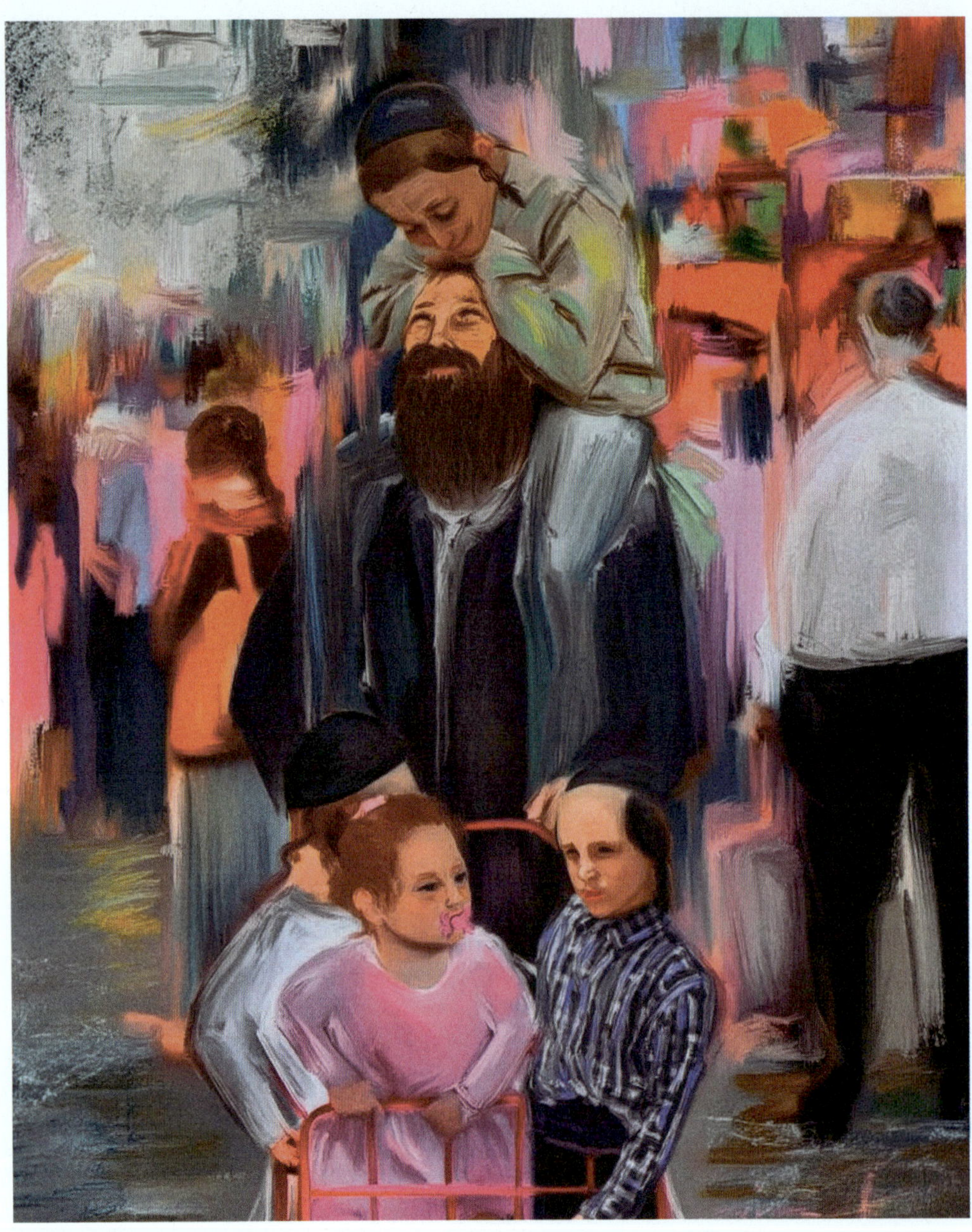

**FULL HANDS FULL HEART (DETAIL)**
Shani Levin, mixed media on canvas, 2020

**TEXT 15**

## Meaningful Belonging

Emily Esfahani Smith, "The Secret to a Meaningful Life is Meaningful Relationships," www.gottman.com

If you ask people what their most significant sources of meaning in life are, they, perhaps unsurprisingly, list their close relationships. . . . That's because one of the pillars of a meaningful life is a sense of belonging. . . .

When people feel like they belong, according to psychologists Mark Leary and Roy Baumeister, it's because . . . they are in relationships with others based on mutual care.

**EMILY ESFAHANI SMITH**

Writer. Emily Esfahani Smith received her master's degree in positive psychology from the University of Pennsylvania, and she is currently a doctoral candidate in clinical psychology at Catholic University. Her writing focuses on the human search for meaning, and she is best known for her book, *The Power of Meaning*.

**TEXT 16A**

## "Living Being"

Genesis 2:7

וַיִּיצֶר ה' אֱלֹקִים אֶת הָאָדָם עָפָר מִן הָאֲדָמָה, וַיִּפַּח
בְּאַפָּיו נִשְׁמַת חַיִּים, וַיְהִי הָאָדָם לְנֶפֶשׁ חַיָּה.

G-d formed the human from the dust of the earth, and He breathed into his nostrils the breath of life, and the human became a living being.

TEXT 16B

## “Speaking Spirit”

Onkelos, ad loc.

וּבְרָא ה' אֱלֹקִים יָת אָדָם עַפְרָא מִן אַרְעָא, וּנְפַח
בְּאַפּוֹהִי נִשְׁמְתָא דְחַיֵי, וַהֲוָת בְּאָדָם לְרוּחַ מְמַלְלָא.

G-d created man, dust from the earth, and He breathed into his nostrils a soul of life; and the human became a speaking spirit.

**ONKELOS**
**C. 35–120 CE**

Famous convert to Judaism in Mishnaic times. According to traditional sources, he was a prominent Roman nobleman and a nephew of the Roman emperor Titus. He is the author of *Targum Unkelos*, an Aramaic translation of the Bible. His *Targum* is an exposition of the interpretation of the Torah, as received by Rabbi Eliezer and Rabbi Yehoshua.

TEXT 17

## Social Humans

Maimonides, *Guide for the Perplexed* 2:40

הָאָדָם מְדִינִי בְּטֶבַע, וְשֶׁטִבְעוֹ שֶׁיִהְיֶה מִתְקַבֵּץ. וְאֵינוֹ
כִּשְׁאַר בַּעֲלֵי הַחַיִים אֲשֶׁר אֵין לוֹ הֶכְרֵחַ לְהִתְקַבֵּץ . . .
וְטִבְעוֹ צָרִיךְ אֶל הַקִיבּוּץ צוֹרֶךְ הֶכְרֵחִי.

Human beings are social by nature, and their nature compels them to gather together with others. They are not like other living creatures, which have no necessity to congregate. . . . Rather, their nature requires social gathering as an absolute necessity.

**RABBI MOSHE BEN MAIMON (MAIMONIDES, RAMBAM)**
**1135–1204**

Halachist, philosopher, author, and physician. Maimonides was born in Córdoba, Spain. After the conquest of Córdoba by the Almohads, he fled Spain and eventually settled in Cairo, Egypt. There, he became the leader of the Jewish community and served as court physician to the vizier of Egypt. He is most noted for authoring the *Mishneh Torah*, an encyclopedic arrangement of Jewish law; and for his philosophical work, *Guide for the Perplexed*. His rulings on Jewish law are integral to the formation of Halachic consensus.

**EXERCISE 1.6**

**What relationships are you currently in that are fulfilling and that provide you with meaning?**

**What relationships can you cultivate, create, or mend to provide you with more meaning?**

**What are some ways to implement these improvements in your life?**

## KEY POINTS

1. Although we live in an era of unprecedented prosperity, depression, anxiety, and substance abuse have reached record levels globally. One of the root causes of the current mental health crisis epidemic is a lack of meaning, a feeling that life is an exercise in futility.

2. We feel meaningful—complete and settled—when we act in ways that are aligned with our core, and we lack meaning when we suffer from misalignment.

3. Based on the Torah's comparison of humans to trees, we identified four qualities that define our identities: growth, productivity, helping others, and genuine relationships.

4. We humans are defined by our capacity for growth. We are distinguished from animals in our capacity to control our instincts and work on ourselves to grow and improve. When we are growing, we are expressing our essential humanity, and thus we feel complete.

5. The mark of our success is not only what we are but what we produce. We have a deep human need to be a contributor, not a person who is dependent on the largesse of others.

6 The desire and need to give to others is hardwired into our human identity, and we can only feel fulfilled when we are benefiting the world around us.

7 Jewish thought has always described the human being as a communicator, capable of connecting with others deeply and spiritually. Tapping into this deepest part of our being provides us with an incredible sense of meaning.

## The Book of Ecclesiastes: An Overview

King Solomon, the wisest man to ever live, wrote three books included in the Scriptures: Song of Songs (Shir Hashirim), a poetic and allegorical description of the romance between G-d and the Jewish nation; Proverbs (Mishlei), a collection of wisdom and practical guidance for life; and Ecclesiastes (Kohelet), his reflections on the nature of existence.

While there is debate about the precise order in which Solomon wrote these three books, there is a consensus that Ecclesiastes was his final work.

The general theme that runs through Ecclesiastes's twelve chapters is the search for lasting meaning in a fleeting world. Solomon describes a search for meaning, suggesting and then disqualifying a range of options including wisdom, pleasure, joy, and wealth. Along the way Solomon offers profound advice for navigating life and handling its difficulties.

The book concludes with Solomon's final conclusion that the meaning of life is reverence for G-d and observance of His commandments.

Many communities have the custom of reading the book of Ecclesiastes publicly on the Shabbat that occurs during the intermediate days of Sukkot. This image is from the Tripartite Machzor, an illuminated manuscript created in Southern Germany, c. 1320, containing the liturgy for all of the festivals. It shows the first page of the book of Ecclesiastes with a decorated opening word panel, accompanied by the commentary of Rabbi Yosef Kara.

The British Library (London, U.K.)

The internal structure of Ecclesiastes is difficult to clearly define. The Hebrew *Daat Mikra* commentary proposes a division into thirteen units:

1. **Introduction**
   1:1–11
2. **Kohelet's personal experiment that taught him all is futile**
   1:12–2:26
3. **The human's relationship to what is Above and what is below**
   3:1–22
4. **Injustice and corruption in human society**
   4:1–16
5. **Guidance for people ascending to the Temple**
   4:17–5:7
6. **Critique of the pursuit of wealth**
   5:8–6:9
7. **A collection of wise sayings**
   6:10–7:14
8. **No human is perfect, but the righteous and wicked receive their just deserts.**
   7:15–8:17
9. **The fate of all humans is in G-d's hands, so one should rejoice in their lot.**
   9:1–18
10. **A collection of wise sayings on opposites: the wise and the foolish, etc.**
    10:1–20
11. **Encouragement for people who work the land**
    11:1–6
12. **The joys of youth and the frailty of old age**
    11:7–12:7
13. **Conclusion: the essence of Kohelet's teachings**
    12:8–14

Some of the sages wished to exclude Ecclesiastes from the canon of Scripture because some of its verses appear to contradict each other. However, they ultimately decided that the value of the religious messages it contains outweighs its internal difficulties, and the Talmud offers resolutions for the apparent contradictions (Shabbat 30b).

In the book of Ecclesiastes, King Solomon is referred to as "Kohelet." The Hebrew root of this word is k-h-l, which means "gathering," and Rashi (Ecclesiastes 1:1) gives two explanations for why Solomon was referred to with this name:

1. King Solomon gathered many branches of wisdom together.
2. King Solomon would teach his wisdom at public gatherings.

The English name Ecclesiastes is derived from the Greek word for a public preacher, which accords with the second explanation.

## SELECTED VERSES FROM ECCLESIASTES

4:9–10

**Two are better than one, since they have good reward for their labor. If either of them falls down, one can help the other up. But woe to anyone who falls and has no one to help them up.**

4:13

**Better a poor and wise child than an old and foolish king who no longer knows how to be cautious.**

5:1

**Do not be rash with your mouth and do not be hasty in your heart to utter anything before G-d. For G-d is in Heaven and you are on earth, so let your words be few.**

5:11

**The sleep of a laborer is sweet, whether they eat little or much, but as for the rich, their abundance permits them no sleep.**

5:18

**When G-d gives someone wealth and possessions, and the ability to enjoy them—to take their portion and rejoice in their toil—this is a gift of G-d.**

7:5

It is better to listen to the rebuke of a wise person than to listen to the song of fools.

7:8

The end of a matter is better than its beginning, and patience is better than pride.

9:9

Enjoy life with your wife whom you love, all the days of this futile life that G-d has given you under the sun—all your futile days. For this is your lot in life and in your toilsome labor under the sun.

10:8–9

Whoever digs a pit will fall into it; whoever breaks through a wall will be bitten by a snake. Whoever quarries stones will be injured by them; whoever splits logs will be endangered by them.

10:12

Words from the mouth of the wise find favor, but fools are consumed by their own lips.

11:1–2

Cast your bread on the surface of the water, for after many days you will receive a return. Divide your resources into seven and even to eight, as you do not know what evil may come upon the earth.

11:6

Sow your seed in the morning, and at evening do not rest your hand, for you do not know which will succeed, whether this or that, or whether both will do equally well.

12:7

The dust returns to the ground it came from, and the spirit returns to G-d Who gave it.

12:13–14

Here is the end of the matter, after everything is considered: Revere G-d and keep His commandments—because that's what it means to be human. For G-d will bring every deed into judgment, including every hidden thing, whether it is good or evil.

## Psychology References

Miller, L., et al. (2012). Religiosity and major depression in adults at high risk: A ten-year prospective study, *American Journal of Psychiatry,* vol. 169, Number 1, 89–94.

Luthar, S. S., et al. (2013). "I can, therefore I must": Fragility in the upper-middle classes. *Development and Psychopathology*, 25 (issue 4, pt. 2), 1529–1549.

Verdoodt, K., et al. (2024). Personal growth initiative across the life span: a systematic review protocol of quantitative studies using the Personal Growth Initiative Scale-II. *Systematic Reviews*, 13(1), 127.

Zun, J., et al. (2024). Factors correlated with personal growth initiative among college students: A meta-analysis, *Heliyon*, vol. 10, issue 7, 2024.

Nigg, J. T. (2017). Annual research review: On the relations among self-regulation, self-control, executive functioning, effortful control, cognitive control, impulsivity, risk-taking, and inhibition for developmental psychopathology. *Journal of Child Psychology and Psychiatry,* 58: 361–383.

Guthrie, D., et al. (2025). Interpersonal mattering and the experience of meaning in life. *The Journal of Positive Psychology*, 20(1), 136–150.

Martela F., & Pessi A. B. (2018). Significant work is about self-realization and broader purpose: Defining the key dimensions of meaningful work. *Frontiers in Psychology* 2018; 9:363.

O'Donnell, M. B., et al. (2014). You, me, and meaning: an integrative review of connections between relationships and meaning in life. *Journal of Psychology in Africa*, 24(1), 44–50.

# LESSON 2

**WHEN MEANING IS NOT TANGIBLE (DETAIL)**
Berit Engen, woven tapestry, linen yarn, Oak Park, Illinois, 2020

## TO MAKE OR NOT TO MAKE MEANING

*When life lacks luster, should we invent a more meaningful way of seeing things? Or is there already a purpose hiding in plain sight?*

## I. INTRODUCTION

Welcome to Lesson Two of *The Kabbalah of Meaning*.

Before we start with today's topic, let's do a fun exercise:

**EXERCISE 2.1**

**Examine the objects in these two images.**
**Can you figure out their functions?**

## II. ECCLESIASTES REVISITED

We started the previous lesson with reading the first verses of the book of Ecclesiastes, in which King Solomon laments the futility of all existence. All is futile, he proclaims; life is, after all, fleeting and meaningless.

King Solomon didn't just make this statement off the cuff. He said it after experimenting with every type of pleasure in an attempt to find joy. After everything he tried, something was still missing.

Depiction of King Solomon, marginal detail at the end of the book of Exodus in The Coburg [Bavaria] Pentateuch, British Library, London, c. 1396

TEXT 1A

## Solomon's Experiment

Ecclesiastes 2:4–11

הִגְדַּלְתִּי מַעֲשָׂי, בָּנִיתִי לִי בָּתִּים, נָטַעְתִּי לִי כְּרָמִים.

עָשִׂיתִי לִי גַּנּוֹת וּפַרְדֵּסִים וְנָטַעְתִּי בָהֶם עֵץ כָּל פֶּרִי.

עָשִׂיתִי לִי בְּרֵכוֹת מָיִם לְהַשְׁקוֹת מֵהֶם יַעַר צוֹמֵחַ עֵצִים.

קָנִיתִי עֲבָדִים וּשְׁפָחוֹת וּבְנֵי בַיִת הָיָה לִי; גַּם מִקְנֶה בָקָר וָצֹאן הַרְבֵּה הָיָה לִי, מִכֹּל שֶׁהָיוּ לְפָנַי בִּירוּשָׁלָם.

כָּנַסְתִּי לִי גַּם כֶּסֶף וְזָהָב וּסְגֻלַּת מְלָכִים וְהַמְּדִינוֹת; עָשִׂיתִי לִי שָׁרִים וְשָׁרוֹת וְתַעֲנֻגוֹת בְּנֵי הָאָדָם, שִׁדָּה וְשִׁדּוֹת.

וְגָדַלְתִּי וְהוֹסַפְתִּי מִכֹּל שֶׁהָיָה לְפָנַי בִּירוּשָׁלָם; אַף חָכְמָתִי עָמְדָה לִּי.

וְכֹל אֲשֶׁר שָׁאֲלוּ עֵינַי לֹא אָצַלְתִּי מֵהֶם, לֹא מָנַעְתִּי אֶת לִבִּי מִכָּל שִׂמְחָה כִּי לִבִּי שָׂמֵחַ מִכָּל עֲמָלִי, וְזֶה הָיָה חֶלְקִי מִכָּל עֲמָלִי.

וּפָנִיתִי אֲנִי בְּכָל מַעֲשַׂי שֶׁעָשׂוּ יָדַי וּבֶעָמָל שֶׁעָמַלְתִּי לַעֲשׂוֹת, וְהִנֵּה הַכֹּל הֶבֶל וּרְעוּת רוּחַ, וְאֵין יִתְרוֹן תַּחַת הַשָּׁמֶשׁ.

I amassed great wealth. I built homes, planted vineyards.

I designed gardens and orchards filled with every kind of fruit tree.

**ECCLESIASTES**

Biblical book. Written by King Solomon, Ecclesiastes is part of the Writings section of the Tanach. Addressing the existential question of the meaning of life, Ecclesiastes exposes the futility of materialism, concluding that Divine worship and *mitzvah* observance is the only true meaning of life. This book is traditionally read in many communities during the holiday of Sukkot.

I made reservoirs to water entire groves of trees.

I acquired male and female servants, and
had more cattle—herds and flocks—than
anyone before me in Jerusalem.

I piled up silver and gold and the treasures
of kings and provinces. I brought in male
and female singers, and every luxury people
could desire—chests and chests of it.

I became wealthier than anyone who came before
me in Jerusalem—and I still had my wisdom.

I didn't hold back from anything my eyes
wanted. I didn't deny myself any pleasure. I
took joy in everything I achieved. But in the
end, that joy was all I really got from it.

Then I looked back at all I had worked for,
everything I had built and gained—and
it was all pointless. Just chasing the wind.
Nothing truly lasting under the sun.

TEXT 1B

## Solomon's Experiment

Ibid., verses 12–17

וּפָנִיתִי אֲנִי לִרְאוֹת חָכְמָה וְהוֹלֵלוֹת וְסִכְלוּת . . .

וְרָאִיתִי אָנִי שֶׁיֵּשׁ יִתְרוֹן לַחָכְמָה מִן
הַסִּכְלוּת כִּיתְרוֹן הָאוֹר מִן הַחֹשֶׁךְ.

הֶחָכָם עֵינָיו בְּרֹאשׁוֹ, וְהַכְּסִיל בַּחֹשֶׁךְ הוֹלֵךְ. וְיָדַעְתִּי
גַם אָנִי שֶׁמִּקְרֶה אֶחָד יִקְרֶה אֶת כֻּלָּם.

וְאָמַרְתִּי אֲנִי בְּלִבִּי, כְּמִקְרֵה הַכְּסִיל גַּם אֲנִי יִקְרֵנִי, וְלָמָּה
חָכַמְתִּי אֲנִי אָז יֹתֵר? וְדִבַּרְתִּי בְלִבִּי שֶׁגַּם זֶה הָבֶל.

כִּי אֵין זִכְרוֹן לֶחָכָם עִם הַכְּסִיל לְעוֹלָם, בְּשֶׁכְּבָר הַיָּמִים
הַבָּאִים, הַכֹּל נִשְׁכָּח, וְאֵיךְ יָמוּת הֶחָכָם עִם הַכְּסִיל?

וְשָׂנֵאתִי אֶת הַחַיִּים כִּי רַע עָלַי הַמַּעֲשֶׂה שֶׁנַּעֲשָׂה
תַּחַת הַשָּׁמֶשׁ, כִּי הַכֹּל הֶבֶל וּרְעוּת רוּחַ.

I turned my thoughts to understanding wisdom—and also madness and foolishness. . . .

I saw that wisdom is better than foolishness, just as light is better than darkness.

A wise person sees where they are going, but a fool stumbles in the dark. But I also realized that the same fate awaits them both.

So I thought: "If I'll end up just like the
fool, what's the point of being wise?" And
I saw that this too is meaningless.

Because neither the wise nor the foolish are remembered
for long. In time, both are forgotten. And in the
end, the wise person dies just like the fool.

That made me hate life. Everything happening under
the sun seemed so pointless—just chasing the wind.

**ABSTRACT PORTRAIT**
Zvi Mairovitch (Poland, 1911–1974, Israel), oil on canvas, Israel

**TEXT 2**

## Meaningless World

Nachmanides, Sermon on Ecclesiastes,
published in *Kitvei Ramban*, vol. 1, pp. 182–183

"הֲבֵל הֲבָלִים אָמַר קֹהֶלֶת הֲבֵל הֲבָלִים הַכֹּל הָבֶל" - אִלּוּ אָדָם אַחֵר אָמַר הֲבֵל הֲבָלִים הַכֹּל הָבֶל הָיִינוּ אוֹמְרִים לֹא אָסַף מִיָּמָיו שְׁתֵּי פְּרוּטוֹת וְהוּא פִּירֵת בְּמָמוֹנוֹ שֶׁל עוֹלָם וְאוֹמֵר הֲבֵל הֲבָלִים? אֶלָּא שְׁלֹמֹה, לְפִי שֶׁכָּתוּב בּוֹ "וַיִּתֵּן הַמֶּלֶךְ אֶת הַכֶּסֶף בִּירוּשָׁלַםִ כָּאֲבָנִים" (מְלָכִים א, י, כז), נָאֶה לוֹ לוֹמַר "הֲבֵל הֲבָלִים" . . .

וְהִנֵּה שְׁלֹמֹה הַשַּׁלִּיט הַיָּכוֹל הֶחָכָם חִבֵּר כָּל הַסֵּפֶר הַזֶּה לִהְיוֹת מַהֲבִּיל כָּל הָעוֹלָם וְלֵאמֹר לָנוּ כִּי הַכֹּל הֶבֶל גָּמוּר.

"Futility of futilities, said Kohelet; futility of futilities, all is futile" (ECCLESIASTES 1:2). If another person had said this, we would have said: They never amassed even two coins in their life, yet they speak about the wealth of the world and declare it futility? But Solomon, about whom it is written, "The king made silver in Jerusalem as abundant as stones" (I KINGS 10:27), is indeed suited to render all as "futility of futilities." . . .

Behold, Solomon—the ruler, the powerful one, the wise—authored this entire book to render the whole world as meaningless and to tell us that everything is utterly futile.

**RABBI MOSHE BEN NACHMAN (NACHMANIDES, RAMBAN) 1194–1270**

Scholar, philosopher, author, and physician. Nachmanides was born in Spain and served as leader of Iberian Jewry. In 1263, he was summoned by King James of Aragon to a public disputation with Pablo Cristiani, a Jewish apostate. Though Nachmanides was the clear victor of the debate, he had to flee Spain because of the resulting persecution. He moved to Israel and helped reestablish communal life in Jerusalem. He authored a classic commentary on the Pentateuch and a commentary on the Talmud.

**TEXT 3**

## Questions of Meaning

Leo Tolstoy (Aylmer Maude, tr.), *A Confession* (Mineola, N.Y.: Dover Publications, 2012), pp. 13–14

Five years ago, something very strange began to happen to me. At first I experienced moments of perplexity and arrest of life, as though I did not know what to do or how to live; and I felt lost and became dejected. But this passed and I went on living as before. Then these moments of perplexity began to recur oftener and oftener, and always in the same form.

They were always expressed by the questions: What's it for? What does it lead to? . . .

I understood that it was no casual indisposition, but something very important, and if these questions constantly repeated themselves, they would have to be answered. And I tried to answer them. The questions seemed such stupid, simple, childish questions; but as soon as I touched them and tried to solve them, I at once became convinced, (1) that they are not childish and stupid, but the most important and profound of life's questions; and (2) that, try as I would, I could not solve them. Before occupying myself with my Samara estate, the education of my son, or the writing of a book, I had to know ***why*** I was doing it. As long as I did not know why, I could do nothing, and could not

**LEO TOLSTOY**
**1828–1910**

Writer. Born to an aristocratic family in the Tula region, Russia, Leo Tolstoy served in the Russian army during the Crimean War, an experience that turned him into an anarchist. He is best known for his acclaimed novels *War and Peace* and *Anna Karenina*. His ideas on nonviolent resistance had a profound impact on such pivotal figures as Mahatma Gandhi and Martin Luther King, Jr.

live. Amid the thoughts of estate management which greatly occupied me at that time, the question would suddenly occur to me: "Well you have 6,000 ***desyatinas*** of land in Samara Government with 300 horses, and what next?" . . . And I was quite disconcerted, and did not know what to think. Or when considering my plans for the education of my children, I would say to myself: "What for?" . . . Or when thinking of the fame my works would bring me, I said to myself, "Very well; you will be more famous than Gogol or Pushkin or Shakespeare or Molière, or than all the writers in the world—and what of it?" And I could find no reply at all.

**THE WINDOW SEAT**
Alfred Aaron Wolmark (1877–1961), oil on canvas, London, England, 1909

## III. ON PURPOSE

The story of Mordecai and Esther provides us with a deeper perspective. Beyond meaning, it pushes us to ask what our *purpose* is.

**TEXT 4A**

### Mordecai's Message

Esther 4:8–14

וְאֶת פַּתְשֶׁגֶן כְּתָב הַדָּת אֲשֶׁר נִתַּן בְּשׁוּשָׁן לְהַשְׁמִידָם
נָתַן לוֹ לְהַרְאוֹת אֶת אֶסְתֵּר, וּלְהַגִּיד לָהּ וּלְצַוּוֹת עָלֶיהָ
לָבוֹא אֶל הַמֶּלֶךְ לְהִתְחַנֶּן לוֹ וּלְבַקֵּשׁ מִלְּפָנָיו עַל עַמָּהּ.

וַיָּבוֹא הֲתָךְ, וַיַּגֵּד לְאֶסְתֵּר אֵת דִּבְרֵי מָרְדֳּכָי.

וַתֹּאמֶר אֶסְתֵּר לַהֲתָךְ וַתְּצַוֵּהוּ אֶל מָרְדֳּכָי:

"כָּל עַבְדֵי הַמֶּלֶךְ וְעַם מְדִינוֹת הַמֶּלֶךְ יוֹדְעִים אֲשֶׁר
כָּל אִישׁ וְאִשָּׁה אֲשֶׁר יָבוֹא אֶל הַמֶּלֶךְ אֶל הֶחָצֵר
הַפְּנִימִית אֲשֶׁר לֹא יִקָּרֵא אַחַת דָּתוֹ לְהָמִית, לְבַד
מֵאֲשֶׁר יוֹשִׁיט לוֹ הַמֶּלֶךְ אֶת שַׁרְבִיט הַזָּהָב וְחָיָה. וַאֲנִי
לֹא נִקְרֵאתִי לָבוֹא אֶל הַמֶּלֶךְ זֶה שְׁלוֹשִׁים יוֹם".

וַיַּגִּידוּ לְמָרְדֳּכָי אֵת דִּבְרֵי אֶסְתֵּר.

וַיֹּאמֶר מָרְדֳּכַי לְהָשִׁיב אֶל אֶסְתֵּר: "אַל תְּדַמִּי
בְנַפְשֵׁךְ לְהִמָּלֵט בֵּית הַמֶּלֶךְ מִכָּל הַיְּהוּדִים.

"כִּי אִם הַחֲרֵשׁ תַּחֲרִישִׁי בָּעֵת הַזֹּאת, רֶוַח וְהַצָּלָה יַעֲמוֹד
לַיְּהוּדִים מִמָּקוֹם אַחֵר וְאַתְּ וּבֵית אָבִיךְ תֹּאבֵדוּ . . .".

**BOOK OF ESTHER**

The biblical account of the Purim story. By special request of Esther of the "Men of the Great Assembly," this book was included in the biblical canon. The book of Esther is read from a scroll twice on the holiday of Purim, the holiday that commemorates the Jews' victory over their antisemitic enemies.

Mordecai gave Hatach a copy of the written decree that had been circulated in Shushan, instructing him to show it to Esther and to urge her to go before the king—to plead with him and beg for the lives of her people.

Hatach went and delivered Mordecai's message to Esther.

Esther then said to Hatach and instructed him to relay her words to Mordecai:

"All the king's servants and the people of the king's provinces know that anyone—man or woman—who enters the king's inner court without being summoned is subject to death, unless the king extends his golden scepter, granting permission to live. And I have not been summoned to the king in thirty days."

Esther's message was conveyed to Mordecai.

Mordecai sent back this reply to Esther: "Don't imagine that you, of all the Jews, will escape just because you're in the palace.

"If you remain silent at this moment, relief and deliverance will come for the Jews from another source, but you and your father's house will perish. . . ."

**TEXT 4B**

## Just Such a Time

Ibid., verse 14

"... וּמִי יוֹדֵעַ אִם לְעֵת כָּזֹאת הִגַּעַתְּ לַמַּלְכוּת?"

"... And who knows—perhaps you became queen for just such a time as this."

**TEXT 4C**

## Esther's Response

Ibid., verses 15–16

וַתֹּאמֶר אֶסְתֵּר לְהָשִׁיב אֶל מָרְדֳּכָי:

"לֵךְ כְּנוֹס אֶת כָּל הַיְּהוּדִים הַנִּמְצְאִים בְּשׁוּשָׁן
וְצוּמוּ עָלַי וְאַל תֹּאכְלוּ וְאַל תִּשְׁתּוּ שְׁלֹשֶׁת יָמִים
לַיְלָה וָיוֹם, גַּם אֲנִי וְנַעֲרֹתַי אָצוּם כֵּן. וּבְכֵן אָבוֹא אֶל
הַמֶּלֶךְ אֲשֶׁר לֹא כַדָּת, וְכַאֲשֶׁר אָבַדְתִּי אָבָדְתִּי".

Esther said to reply to Mordecai:

"Go, gather all the Jews who are found in Shushan, and fast for me; do not eat and do not drink for three days, night and day. I, too, along with my maidens, will fast likewise. And then I will go to the king, though it is against the law; and if I perish, I perish."

FIGURE 2.1

## Meaning vs. Purpose

| | SEQUENCE | | VALUE | |
|---|---|---|---|---|
| MEANING | Person >> Meaning | I happen to exist; let me live a meaningful life. | Arbitrary | We can attribute any meaning to life. |
| PURPOSE | Purpose >> Person | Something is needed; I am introduced to fill that need. | Inherent | There is an objective purpose to life. |

Purim scene: Queen Esther and Mordecai approaching King Ahasuerus, tapestry, silk and wool, Belgium, Nazmiyal Collection, New York, 1580

**TEXT 5**

## The Meaning of Religion

Rabbi Lord Jonathan Sacks,
"The Limits of Secularism," *Standpoint Magazine*,
January/February 2012

Think about it: every function that was once performed by religion can now be done by something else. In other words, if you want to explain the world, you don't need Genesis; you have science. If you want to control the world, you don't need prayer; you have technology. If you want to prosper, you don't necessarily seek G-d's blessing; you have the global economy. You want to control power, you no longer need prophets; you have liberal democracy and elections.

If you're ill, you don't need a priest; you can go to a doctor. If you feel guilty, you don't have to confess; you can go to a psychotherapist instead. If you're depressed, you don't need faith; you can take a pill. If you still need salvation, you can go to today's cathedrals, the shopping centres of Britain—or as one American writer calls them, weapons of mass consumption. Religion seems superfluous, redundant, de trop. Why then does it survive?

My answer is simple. Religion survives because it answers three questions that every reflective person must ask. Who am I? Why am I here? How then shall I live?

**RABBI LORD JONATHAN SACKS 1948–2020**

Chief Rabbi of the United Kingdom from 1991 through 2013. Rabbi Sacks attended Cambridge University and received his doctorate from King's College, London. A prolific and influential author, his books include *Will We Have Jewish Grandchildren?* and *The Dignity of Difference.* He received the Jerusalem Prize in 1995 for his contributions to enhancing Jewish life in the Diaspora, was knighted and made a life peer in 2005, and became Baron Sacks of Aldridge in 2009.

**TEXT 6**

## Personal Purpose

Rabbi Avraham Yitzchak Hakohen Kook,
*Siddur Olat Re'iyah* 2:356

לִפְנֵי שֶׁנּוֹצַרְתִּי, כָּל אוֹתוֹ הַזְּמַן הַבִּלְתִּי מוּגְבָּל שֶׁמֵּעוֹלָם עַד שֶׁנּוֹצַרְתִּי, וַדַּאי לֹא הָיָה דָּבָר בָּעוֹלָם שֶׁהָיָה צָרִיךְ לִי. כִּי אִם הָיִיתִי חָסֵר בִּשְׁבִיל אֵיזוֹ תַּכְלִית וְהַשְׁלָמָה הָיִיתִי נוֹצָר. וְכֵיוָן שֶׁלֹּא נוֹצַרְתִּי עַד אוֹתוֹ הַזְּמַן הוּא אוֹת, שֶׁלֹּא הָיִיתִי כְּדַאי עַד אָז לְהִבָּרְאוֹת, וְלֹא הָיָה בִּי צוֹרֶךְ כִּי אִם לָעֵת כָּזֹאת שֶׁנִּבְרֵאתִי, מִפְּנֵי שֶׁהִגִּיעָה הַשָּׁעָה שֶׁאֲנִי צָרִיךְ לְמַלֵּא אֵיזֶה דָּבָר לְהַשְׁלָמַת הַמְּצִיאוּת.

Before I was created—during all the limitless time that came before—there was nothing in the world that required me. Had I been needed for any purpose or task, I would have existed earlier. The fact that I wasn't created until that specific moment is proof that there was no need for me until then. My existence was not necessary—until it was. And when the time came, I was brought into the world to fulfill a role, to contribute something essential to the perfection of existence.

**RABBI AVRAHAM YITZCHAK HAKOHEN KOOK 1864–1935**

Rabbi, author, and thinker. Born in Latvia, Rabbi Kook served as a rabbi in eastern European communities before immigrating to Israel in 1904 to serve as the rabbi of Jaffa. In 1917, he became the first Ashkenazic chief rabbi of pre-state Israel, and he was a leading figure in the religious Zionist movement. Rabbi Kook wrote many books on Jewish thought and law—including *Orot Hakodesh*—most of which were published posthumously.

**FIGURE 2.2**

## Meaning vs. Purpose

| | MEANING | PURPOSE |
|---|---|---|
| **BEGINS** | **With me:** I am looking for something meaningful, and I determine what "meaningful" is. | **Before me:** It is the reason I am here (in general, or in any given situation). |
| **ENDS** | **With me:** Success is determined by whether or not I found it to be meaningful. | **Beyond me:** Success is determined by whether or not the need was filled. |

**TEXT 7**

## "Why Are You Needed?"

Rabbi Yosef Yitzchak Schneersohn,
*Igrot Kodesh* 3, p. 439

וַיָּבוֹא לִכְבוֹד קְדוּשַּׁת רַבֵּינוּ הַגָּדוֹל וַיִּשְׁפּוֹךְ אֶת לְבָבוֹ בְּרוֹב בְּכִי וּבְצַעַר פְּנִימִי, בְּאָמְרוֹ, אִם יִסְרוֹ הַשֵּׁם יִתְבָּרֵךְ וְחַס וְשָׁלוֹם גָּזַר עָלָיו עֲנִיּוּת, מַצְדִּיק עָלָיו אֶת הַדִּין. אֲבָל אֵיךְ אֶפְשָׁר הַדָּבָר אֲשֶׁר חַס וְשָׁלוֹם יִשָּׁאֵר בַּעַל חוֹב וְלֹא יְשַׁלֵּם אוֹ שֶׁלֹּא יְקַיֵּים מוֹצָא שְׂפָתָיו אֲשֶׁר הִבְטִיחַ לִקְרוֹבָיו וּבְנֵי מִשְׁפַּחְתּוֹ וְגַם נִשּׂוּאֵי בְּנוֹתָיו בִּכְלָל? הֲלֹא הִבְטִיחַ לָהֶם בִּהְיוֹתוֹ עָשִׁיר, אֲשֶׁר עַל פִּי תּוֹרָתֵינוּ הַקְּדוֹשָׁה הָיָה לוֹ רְשׁוּת לְהַבְטִיחַ, וְאִם עַתָּה לֹא יְקַיֵּים הַבְטָחָתוֹ הֲוֵי חִילּוּל הַשֵּׁם.

וַיִּבְכֶּה בִּמְרִירוּת עֲצוּמָה עַל הָעוֹנֶשׁ הַגָּדוֹל, רַחֲמָנָא לִיצְלַן, אֲשֶׁר מַעֲנִישִׁים אוֹתוֹ מִן הַשָּׁמַיִם בְּחֵטְא שֶׁל חִילּוּל הַשֵּׁם,

**RABBI YOSEF YITZCHAK SCHNEERSOHN (RAYATZ, FRIERDIKER REBBE, PREVIOUS REBBE) 1880–1950**

Chasidic rebbe, prolific writer, and Jewish activist. Rabbi Yosef Yitzchak, the 6th leader of the Chabad movement, actively promoted Jewish religious practice in Soviet Russia and was arrested for these activities. After his release from prison and exile, he settled in Warsaw, Poland, from where he fled Nazi occupation and arrived in New York in 1940. Settling in Brooklyn, Rabbi Schneersohn worked to revitalize American Jewish life. His son-in-law Rabbi Menachem Mendel Schneerson succeeded him as the leader of the Chabad movement.

וַיְעוֹרֵר רַחֲמִים וְתַחֲנוּנִים לִפְנֵי כְּבוֹד קְדוּשַּׁת רַבֵּינוּ הַגָּדוֹל, כִּי יְעוֹרֵר עָלָיו רַחֲמִים רַבִּים מִמְּקוֹר הָרַחֲמִים וְהַחֲסָדִים הָאֲמִיתִּים, כִּי יְשַׁלֵּם הַחוֹבוֹת שֶׁלּוֹ וִיקַיֵּם הַבְטָחָתוֹ, וְאַחַר כָּךְ מְקַבֵּל עָלָיו כָּל הַנִּגְזָר, חַס וְשָׁלוֹם, עָלָיו בָּעֲנִיּוּת.

וַיְסַיֵּים דְּבָרָיו, "רַבִּי! אִיךְ דַאַרְף אָפְּצָאהלִין אַלֶע מַיינֶע חוֹבוֹת, אִיךְ דַאַרְף אָפְּגֶעבִּין אַלֶע קְרוֹבִים אוּן בְּנֵי הַמִּשְׁפָּחָה דָּאס וָואס אִיךְ הָאבּ זֵיי מַבְטִיחַ גֶעוֶועןְ, אוּן אִיךְ דַאַרְף אוֹיסְגֶעבִּין דִי צְוֵויי טֶעכְטֶער וִוי אִיךְ הָאבּ מַבְטִיחַ גֶעוֶוען".

כְּבוֹד קְדוּשַּׁת רַבֵּינוּ הַגָּדוֹל הָיָה נִשְׁעָן עַל אֲצִילֵי יָדָיו הַקְּדוֹשִׁים בִּדְבֵיקוּת עֲצוּמָה וְשָׁמַע תַּחֲנוּנָיו וּבְכִיּוֹתָיו. כַּעֲבוֹר זְמַן נָכוֹן הֵרִים כְּבוֹד קְדוּשַּׁת רַבֵּינוּ הַגָּדוֹל רֹאשׁוֹ הַקָּדוֹשׁ, וְאָמַר בִּדְבֵיקוּת עֲצוּמָה:

"דוּ זָאגְסְט אַלְץ וָואס דוּ דַארְפְסְט, אוֹיף וָואס מִי דַארְף דִיךְ זָאגְסְטוּ גָאר נִיט".

He traveled to the Rebbe, Rabbi Shneur Zalman of Liadi, and poured out his heart with many tears and deep anguish. "If G-d has seen fit to afflict me with poverty, I accept the judgment," he said. "But how can I, G-d forbid, remain in debt and fail to repay? How can I not fulfill the promises I made to my family and relatives? And my daughters' weddings? I made those promises back when I was wealthy. According to our holy Torah, I had every right to make those commitments. If I now fail to keep them, it will be a desecration of G-d's Name."

He cried bitterly over the great punishment that he was being made to endure. With great emotion, he begged the Rebbe to arouse abundant mercy on his behalf from the Source of true compassion and kindness—that he might repay his debts and fulfill his promises. "After that," he said, "I'll accept whatever poverty Heaven has decreed upon me."

He ended his words: "Rebbe, I need to repay all my debts. I need to give my relatives and family members what I promised them. I need to provide for the weddings of my two daughters, as I promised them."

The Rebbe was leaning on his holy arms in deep spiritual absorption, listening to the man's cries and pleas. After some time, the Rebbe lifted his holy head and, still absorbed in that intense spiritual state, said:

"You speak of what you need. But you say nothing about why you are needed."

## IV. THE LIMITATIONS OF THE SYSTEM

Having established that our life has a purpose, we now turn to explore how we can find that purpose.

***HEICHAL SHEL MAALAH***
Yoram Raanan

**TEXT 8**

## Outside Meaning

Rabbi Lord Jonathan Sacks, *The Great Partnership: Science, Religion, and the Search for Meaning* (New York: Schocken Books, 2012), pp. 29–30

Take a game like football. Some hypothetical visitor from a land to which football has not yet penetrated wants to understand this strange ritual which excites so much passion. You explain the rules of the game, what counts as a foul, what constitutes a goal, and so on. "Fine," says the visitor, "I now understand the game. What I don't understand is why you get so excited about it." Here you might have to launch into some larger reflection about games as ritualised conflict, and the role of play in rehearsing skills needed in actual conflict. You might even suggest that ritualised conflict reduces the need for actual conflict: the football pitch as a substitute for the battlefield.

There is an internal logic of the system—the rules of football—but the meaning of the system lies elsewhere, and it can only be understood through some sense of the wider human context in which it is set. To do this you have to step outside the system and see why it was brought into being. There is no way of understanding the meaning of football by merely knowing its rules. They tell you how to play the game, but not why people do so and why they invest in it the passions they do. The internal workings of a system do not explain the place the system holds in human lives.

The meaning of the system lies outside the system. Therefore, the meaning of the universe lies outside the universe. . . . Only something or someone outside the universe can give meaning to the universe.

TEXT 9

## First Torah

*Midrash Tehilim*, Psalms 90:4

אַלְפַּיִם שָׁנָה קָדְמָה תּוֹרָה לִבְרִיָּיתוֹ שֶׁל עוֹלָם.

The Torah's existence precedes the world by two thousand years.

***MIDRASH TEHILIM***

A rabbinic commentary on the book of Psalms. Midrash is the designation of a particular genre of rabbinic literature usually forming a running commentary on specific books of the Bible. This particular Midrash provides textual exegeses and develops and illustrates the principles of the book of Psalms.

## V. THE ONLY SAFE PLACE

We live in a world that constantly urges us to protect ourselves: Take more "me time," set better boundaries, curate our lives for optimal emotional safety. If we can just feel more seen, heard, rested, and in control, the thinking goes, we'll be happy.

And it works—until it doesn't. What is missing?

**ABOVE ALL**
Samuel Bak (b. 1933, Lithuania), oil on canvas, 2020

TEXT 10

## The Fox and the Fish

Talmud, Berachot 61b

פַּעַם אַחַת גָּזְרָה מַלְכוּת הָרְשָׁעָה שֶׁלֹּא יַעַסְקוּ יִשְׂרָאֵל בַּתּוֹרָה. בָּא פַּפּוּס בֶּן יְהוּדָה וּמְצָאוֹ לְרַבִּי עֲקִיבָא שֶׁהָיָה מַקְהִיל קְהִלּוֹת בָּרַבִּים וְעוֹסֵק בַּתּוֹרָה. אָמַר לוֹ:

"עֲקִיבָא, אִי אַתָּה מִתְיָרֵא מִפְּנֵי מַלְכוּת?"

אָמַר לוֹ: אֶמְשׁוֹל לְךָ מָשָׁל,

לְמָה הַדָּבָר דּוֹמֶה – לְשׁוּעָל שֶׁהָיָה מְהַלֵּךְ עַל גַּב הַנָּהָר, וְרָאָה דָּגִים שֶׁהָיוּ מִתְקַבְּצִים מִמָּקוֹם לְמָקוֹם. אָמַר לָהֶם: "מִפְּנֵי מָה אַתֶּם בּוֹרְחִים?"

אָמְרוּ לוֹ: "מִפְּנֵי רְשָׁתוֹת שֶׁמְּבִיאִין עָלֵינוּ בְּנֵי אָדָם".

אָמַר לָהֶם: "רְצוֹנְכֶם שֶׁתַּעֲלוּ לַיַּבָּשָׁה, וְנָדוּר אֲנִי וְאַתֶּם, כְּשֵׁם שֶׁדָּרוּ אֲבוֹתַי עִם אֲבוֹתֵיכֶם?"

אָמְרוּ לוֹ: "אַתָּה הוּא שֶׁאוֹמְרִים עָלֶיךָ פִּקֵּחַ שֶׁבַּחַיּוֹת? לֹא פִּקֵּחַ אַתָּה, אֶלָּא טִפֵּשׁ אַתָּה! וּמָה בִּמְקוֹם חַיּוּתֵנוּ, אָנוּ מִתְיָרְאִין, בִּמְקוֹם מִיתָתֵנוּ – עַל אַחַת כַּמָּה וְכַמָּה".

אַף אֲנַחְנוּ, עַכְשָׁיו שֶׁאָנוּ יוֹשְׁבִים וְעוֹסְקִים בַּתּוֹרָה - שֶׁכָּתוּב בָּהּ: "כִּי הוּא חַיֶּיךָ וְאֹרֶךְ יָמֶיךָ" (דְּבָרִים ל, כ) - כָּךְ, אִם אָנוּ הוֹלְכִים וּמְבַטְּלִים מִמֶּנָּה – עַל אַחַת כַּמָּה וְכַמָּה!

**BABYLONIAN TALMUD**

A literary work of monumental proportions that draws upon the legal, spiritual, intellectual, ethical, and historical traditions of Judaism. The 37 tractates of the Babylonian Talmud contain the teachings of the Jewish sages from the period after the destruction of the 2nd Temple through the 5th century CE. It has served as the primary vehicle for the transmission of the Oral Law and the education of Jews over the centuries; it is the entry point for all subsequent legal, ethical, and theological Jewish scholarship.

Once, the wicked Roman government issued a decree forbidding Jews from studying Torah. Papus ben Yehudah came upon Rabbi Akiva, who was publicly gathering groups and teaching Torah.

He said to him, "Akiva, aren't you afraid of the authorities?"

Rabbi Akiva replied, "Let me tell you a parable.

"A fox was walking along a river and saw fish darting back and forth. He said to them, 'Why are you fleeing?'

"They answered, 'From the nets that people have cast for us.'

"Said the fox, 'Why don't you come up onto dry land and live with me, just as your ancestors lived with mine?'

"The fish said to him, 'Are you the one they call the cleverest of animals? You're not clever—you're foolish! If we're in danger even here, in the place that gives us life, how much more so if we leave it for a place where we can't survive!'

"The same is true for us," Rabbi Akiva concluded. "If we're at risk even while studying Torah—the source of our life, as it says, 'For it is your life and the length of your days' (DEUTERONOMY 30:20)—how much worse would it be if we abandoned it?"

TEXT 11

## The Bottom Line

Ecclesiastes 12:13

סוֹף דָּבָר הַכֹּל נִשְׁמָע אֶת הָאֱלֹקִים יְרָא וְאֶת
מִצְוֹתָיו שְׁמוֹר כִּי זֶה כָּל הָאָדָם.

The end of the matter, after everything is considered: revere G-d and keep His commandments—because that's what it means to be human.

**DANCE**
Aron Rosha,
acrylic, Israel, 2025

## KEY POINTS

1. The question about searching for the meaning of our lives is a distraction. Meaning is subjective: It refers to anything I deem to be enriching, inspiring, and beneficial. There's a more important question we need to answer: What is our *purpose*? Purpose is objective and focuses on what I am needed for at any given moment, irrespective of personal feelings, preferences, and benefits.

2. G-d created us intentionally, so our lives are inherently purposeful. There is a mission that precedes our coming into the world, and Judaism wants us to ask, "What is my purpose?" rather than just "What do I find meaningful?"

3. Purpose isn't dependent on circumstances because if G-d put us in a certain situation, there is certainly purpose in it for us.

4. Purpose can't be discovered from inside the system; it must come from outside the system. Only from beyond existence can we find the purpose for which the entire system was established. The Torah conceptually precedes the world. It is not part of Creation; it is from beyond the system.

5. A society that prioritizes pleasure and freedom, even if pursued through meaningful channels, cannot hold together. With no higher calling and no objective reason for being here, we float freely, and meaning disappears. For us Jews, Torah is the only space where our soul can imbibe life-sustaining purpose.

# Finding Purpose

A collection of texts and stories about finding one's purpose in life.

## TEXTS

RABBI TZADOK HAKOHEN RABINOWITZ, *PERI TZADIK*, SHEKALIM 1

The Talmud teaches that every person must say, "The world was created for me" (Sanhedrin 37a). This is literally true: the entire world was created for each and every person. . . .

This applies to every individual, for each person has something special and unique, on account of which the entire world exists for them and needs them.

RABBI YOSEF YITZCHAK SCHNEERSOHN, CITED IN *HAYOM YOM*, 5 IYAR

The Alter Rebbe [Rabbi Shneur Zalman of Liadi] received the following teaching from the saintly Rabbi Mordechai, who heard it from the Baal Shem Tov:

"A soul can descend into this world and live its seventy or eighty years — just in order to do a favor for a fellow Jew in material matters, and how much more so, in spiritual matters."

RABBI MOSHE CORDOVERO, *SHI'UR KOMAH* 84

How can we know the purpose for which we entered this world? . . . The answer to this question is ingrained in our nature. We experience natural affinity and longing to perform a certain *mitzvah* when that *mitzvah* is critical to the purpose of our creation. Another clue lies in our negative inclination, which puts extra effort into tempting us to commit the very transgression we were put in this world to overcome.

RABBI SHALOM DOVBER SCHNEERSOHN, CITED IN *HAYOM YOM*, 1 CHESHVAN

From the moment that G-d instructed our forefather Abraham, "Go from your land . . ." (Genesis 12:1)—following which it is stated, "Abram kept traveling further southward"—the mystical process of the rectification of the fallen Divine sparks was launched. Subsequently, by decree of Divine providence, individuals travel to the locations in which the Divine sparks that these specific individuals must rectify await their redemption.

Saintly individuals with spiritual vision perceive the locations in which their Divine sparks await their engagement, and they take the initiative to journey to those locations. The rest of us are left in the hands of the primary Cause behind all causes and the ultimate Reason behind all reasons: G-d orchestrates countless apparent causes and circumstances to bring specific individuals to the locations in which their predestined service of rectification is required.

## STORIES

**Based on Rabbi Yosef Yitzchak Schneersohn, *Igrot Kodesh*, vol. 7, pp. 20–21**

A Chasid who worked as a silversmith and watch repairman relocated from the Russian city of Polotzk to Volodymyr, in the Russian interior.

When he next visited his Rebbe, Rabbi Shmuel Schneersohn of Lubavitch, the Rebbe asked him, "Do you have a set time to teach Torah?"

The Chasid replied that he studied privately for an hour each day and also spent time preparing to read the Torah in synagogue, since no one else in town could do it.

He described the Jews of Volodymyr as simple and uneducated. Most didn't even know how to pray. All they could do was answer "Amen" after the prayer leader. Even saying the blessings over the Torah was difficult for them.

The Rebbe asked, "So why did you move there? Why would you leave a Jewish center like Polotzk for a place like Volodymyr?"

The Chasid answered, "I work there as a silversmith and clock repairman. Of course, it pained me to leave my hometown, with its G-d-fearing Jews, two yeshivas, many schools, and synagogues where people pray from dawn until midnight. But I was struggling financially. I even asked the Rebbe's advice at the time, and he approved and gave me his blessing—and thank G-d, that blessing has been fulfilled. I now make a comfortable living in Volodymyr."

The Rebbe responded:

"You're mistaken. G-d didn't send you to Volodymyr for your livelihood. Someone who believes in G-d, in Torah, and in Divine providence must understand: G-d doesn't uproot a Jewish man and his family from a strong Jewish city and send them into a spiritual wilderness just so they can earn a living.

"And your mistake goes even deeper: you think your job is to work with silver and gold and repair watches. That, too, is a big mistake.

"A Jew's true work is Torah and serving G-d. G-d transferred you from Polotzk to Volodymyr so you would positively influence these uneducated Jews in their Judaism.

"Someone who thinks G-d moves Jews from place to place just for a paycheck is lacking in faith. G-d provides sustenance everywhere. What difference does it make if it's Polotzk or Volodymyr?

"I gave you a blessing. But blessings only help when someone does their part. Without action, even a blessing can't help."

**Based on Rabbi Yosef Yitzchak Schneersohn, *Sefer Hasichot* 5704, pp. 154–155**

A wealthy man was traveling on one of his regular business trips, accompanied by his wagon driver. Late Friday afternoon, as the sun was beginning to set, they stopped in a town where no one knew them, planning to stay for Shabbat.

The driver dropped off his employer at the hotel and went to tend to the horses and wagon. The wealthy man rented a room, bathed, changed into his special Shabbat clothes, and headed to the synagogue.

On his way, he passed a man whose wagon was stuck in the mud. Assisting a stranded wagon driver is a biblical *mitzvah*, and not realizing how difficult it would be, the businessman offered to help. Within minutes, he was covered in mud—and worse, he injured himself. He barely managed to limp into synagogue just as prayers began, dirty and in pain.

Meanwhile, the wagon driver had finished his work, dressed for Shabbat, and also made his way to synagogue. Arriving early, he sat down to recite Psalms. Seeing several poor guests gathered there, he invited them to join him for the Shabbat meal, eventually gathering ten people.

After services, the wealthy man returned to his hotel, exhausted and demoralized, while the wagon driver walked home joyfully with his guests.

But the driver's budget didn't match his generous heart. The guests left his home hungry. Here was an experienced coachman, more than capable of pulling wagons from the mud, stretching beyond his means to feed a dozen people. Meanwhile, the wealthy man—whose leftover food could've fed the whole synagogue—had been stuck in a muddy ditch.

When both men eventually passed on and stood before the Heavenly Court, it was ruled that the wagon driver would need to return to this world to fulfill the *mitzvah* of providing roadside assistance, and the businessman would have to return to fulfill the commandment of hosting needy guests. Had the businessman simply asked his driver to help with the wagon, the coachman could have done it far more effectively—and both might have fulfilled their unique life's mission.

Every soul is entrusted with a unique mission—and given the tools to succeed. The real tragedy is spending a lifetime trying everything—except the one thing you were actually meant to do.

## Psychology References

Klausen, S. H., et al. (2021). The many faces of hedonic adaptation. *Philosophical Psychology*, 35(2), 253–278.

Galiani, S., et al. (2018). The half-life of happiness: Hedonic adaptation in the subjective well-being of poor slum dwellers to the satisfaction of basic housing needs, *Journal of the European Economic Association*, vol. 16, issue 4, August 2018, pp. 1189–1233.

Tanzer, J. R. (2019). Developing authentic happiness: Growth curve models to assess lifelong happiness. *The Journal of Positive Psychology*, 16(1), 11–19.

Cutler, J., & Campbell-Meiklejohn, D. (2019). A comparative fMRI meta-analysis of altruistic and strategic decisions to give. *NeuroImage*, 184, 227–241.

Jenkinson, C., et al. (2023). Exploring the effects of volunteering on the social, mental, and physical health of volunteers: An umbrella review. *BMC Public Health*, 23, 821.

Hui, B. P. H., et al. (2020). Kindness makes you happy . . . and vice versa: A meta-analysis of randomized controlled trials of prosocial behavior. *Psychological Bulletin*, 146(12), 1084–1116.

Chen, Y., et al. (2019). Sense of mission and subsequent health and well-being among young adults: An outcome-wide analysis. *American Journal of Epidemiology*, 188(4), 664–673.

THE WALK WITH A PURPOSE (DETAIL)
Berit Engen, woven tapestry, linen yarn, Oak Park, Illinois, 2013

## MEANING IN THE MUNDANE

*Even if it happens every day, daily life needn't feel ordinary. See how every part of the day can be as significant as your highest aspirations.*

## I. DEGREES OF MEANING

In our previous class, we learned how our lives can gain coherence when we discover a unifying purpose. The present class takes this further, searching for meaning even in the routine elements of our daily lives.

**THE ARTIST'S FAMILY (DETAIL)**
Leonid Balaklav, oil on canvas, Israel, 2015

EXERCISE 3.1

## Daily Meaning Reflection

Below is a walk-through of a typical day, along with occasional special events. Your job is to rate how meaningful each activity *usually* feels to you, on a scale of **1 to 5**:

**1 = No meaning**
**5 = Deeply meaningful**

This isn't a productivity test. There are no wrong answers. This is just an honest look at your day-to-day life through the lens of meaning.

### Morning Routine

- Waking up and taking a shower
- Eating breakfast and taking vitamins or medication
- Morning prayer or meditation

### Daytime Work and Tasks

- Doing your primary job (e.g., desk work, teaching, managing, caregiving)
- Preparing meals for yourself or others
- Doing housework (laundry, cleaning, errands)
- Helping someone (a neighbor, friend, or stranger)
- Attending a study session or learning something new

**Physical and Mental Health**

- Exercising or walking
- Choosing healthy meals/snacks during the day
- Taking time to rest or nap if needed

**Social Interactions**

- Having lunch with someone
- Laughing or chatting during a break
- Texting, calling, or messaging friends
- Checking in on someone

**Evening and Leisure**

- Watching a show or attending a concert
- Reading or doing a hobby
- Going outside—walking, gardening, sitting in nature
- Doing something creative (music, painting, writing)

**Spiritual and Reflective Time**

- Evening prayer, meditation, or Torah study
- Doing a *mitzvah* or act of kindness
- Reflecting on your day before bed

### Special Events

- Attending a wedding, bar mitzvah, or other celebration
- Spending Shabbat or a holiday with family or community
- Attending a cause or event that matters to you

### Reflection Prompt

After rating everything, look over your answers. What kinds of activities tend to score highest for you? What patterns do you notice?

## II. IT'S NOT ABOUT ME

To find meaning in the mundane routine, we need to look beyond our mundane selves and mundane world.

**MOMENT OF CLARITY, *VAYIGASH***
Itamar Rubner, oil on board, Jerusalem, 2021

**TEXT 1A**

## “For My Glory”

Avot 6:11

כָּל מַה שֶּׁבָּרָא הַקָּדוֹשׁ בָּרוּךְ הוּא בְּעוֹלָמוֹ, לֹא בְרָאוֹ אֶלָּא לִכְבוֹדוֹ, שֶׁנֶּאֱמַר: "כֹּל הַנִּקְרָא בִשְׁמִי וְלִכְבוֹדִי בְּרָאתִיו יְצַרְתִּיו אַף עֲשִׂיתִיו" (יְשַׁעְיָה מג, ז).

Everything that G-d created in His world, He created only for His glory, as it is stated, “All that is attributed to My name, for My glory I created it, formed it, and made it” (ISAIAH 43:7).

**AVOT**
***(ETHICS OF THE FATHERS; PIRKEI AVOT)***

A 6-chapter work on Jewish ethics that is studied widely by Jewish communities, especially during the summer. The first 5 chapters are from the Mishnah, tractate Avot. Avot differs from the rest of the Mishnah in that it does not focus on legal subjects; it is a collection of the sages’ wisdom on topics related to character development, ethics, healthy living, piety, and the study of Torah.

***BRIAH* CREATION**
David Rakia (Vienna, 1928–2012, Jerusalem), acrylic on paper, Jerusalem, 1996

**TEXT 1B**

## The Sole Purpose

Rabbi Yehudah Loew, *Derech Chayim* 6:11

תַּכְלִית הָאָדָם, וְהוּא . . . תַּכְלִית הַכֹּל, הוּא הַקָּדוֹשׁ בָּרוּךְ הוּא, שֶׁהֲרֵי כָּל הַנִּבְרָאִים לֹא נִבְרְאוּ אֶלָּא לִכְבוֹדוֹ יִתְבָּרֵךְ. וְאִם כֵּן תַּכְלִית הַכֹּל הוּא הַשֵּׁם יִתְבָּרֵךְ, וְאֵין זוּלָתוֹ.

וְכֵן שְׁלֹמֹה הַמֶּלֶךְ עָלָיו הַשָּׁלוֹם . . . סִיֵּים דְּבָרָיו "סוֹף דָּבָר הַכֹּל נִשְׁמָע, אֶת הָאֱלֹקִים יְרָא וְאֶת מִצְוֹתָיו שְׁמוֹר כִּי זֶה כָּל הָאָדָם" (קֹהֶלֶת יב, יג). רָצָה לוֹמַר, כִּי כָּל הָעוֹלָם לֹא נִבְרָא רַק בִּשְׁבִיל זֶה, שֶׁהֲרֵי הַכֹּל נִבְרָא בִּשְׁבִיל הָאָדָם, וְהָאָדָם נִבְרָא שֶׁיְּהֵא יְרֵא אֶת הָאֱלֹקִים וְאֶת מִצְוֹתָיו לִשְׁמוֹר . . .

וּלְפִיכָךְ יַעֲשֶׂה הָאָדָם תַּכְלִיתוֹ דָּבָר זֶה, מֵאַחַר שֶׁכָּל תַּכְלִית הָאָדָם וְכָל הָעוֹלָם לְדָבָר זֶה.

G-d is the purpose of all people and all things, for everything was created to serve His glory. Thus, G-d is the sole purpose, and there is no purpose but for Him.

King Solomon of blessed memory similarly concluded his work: "The end of the matter, after everything has been heard, is to revere G-d and observe His commandments, for this is the entire human" (ECCLESIASTES 12:13). This means that the entire universe was created only for this purpose: the universe was created for

**RABBI YEHUDAH LOEW (MAHARAL OF PRAGUE) 1525–1609**

Talmudist and philosopher. Maharal rose to prominence as leader of the famed Jewish community of Prague. He is the author of more than a dozen works of original philosophic thought, including *Tiferet Yisrael* and *Netzach Yisrael*. He also authored *Gur Aryeh*, a supercommentary to Rashi's biblical commentary; and a commentary on the nonlegal passages of the Talmud. He is buried in the Old Jewish Cemetery of Prague.

humans, and humans were created to revere G-d and observe His commandments. . . .

Considering that this is the sole purpose of all humans and the entire universe, it is fitting that we each make this our sole purpose.

**SHABBAT SHALOM**
Talya Johnson

**TEXT 2**

## Ignoring the Benefits

Maimonides, *Mishneh Torah,*
Laws of Repentance 10:1

אַל יֹאמַר אָדָם: "הֲרֵינִי עוֹשֶׂה מִצְוֹת הַתּוֹרָה וְעוֹסֵק בְּחָכְמָתָהּ כְּדֵי שֶׁאֲקַבֵּל כָּל הַבְּרָכוֹת הַכְּתוּבוֹת בָּהּ אוֹ כְּדֵי שֶׁאֶזְכֶּה לְחַיֵּי הָעוֹלָם הַבָּא. וְאֶפְרֹשׁ מִן הָעֲבֵרוֹת שֶׁהִזְהִירָה תּוֹרָה מֵהֶן כְּדֵי שֶׁאֶנָּצֵל מִן הַקְּלָלוֹת הַכְּתוּבוֹת בַּתּוֹרָה אוֹ כְּדֵי שֶׁלֹּא אֶכָּרֵת מֵחַיֵּי הָעוֹלָם הַבָּא".

אֵין רָאוּי לַעֲבֹד אֶת ה' עַל הַדֶּרֶךְ הַזֶּה, שֶׁהָעוֹבֵד עַל דֶּרֶךְ זֶה הוּא עוֹבֵד מִיִּרְאָה, וְאֵינָהּ מַעֲלַת הַנְּבִיאִים וְלֹא מַעֲלַת הַחֲכָמִים.

One should not say, "I will fulfill the *mitzvot* of the Torah and study its wisdom to receive its many blessings or to merit reward in the World to Come. I will refrain from the sins against which the Torah warns to be spared punishment, or so my soul will not be cut off from life in the World to Come."

It is not fitting to serve G-d in this manner. Those whose service is motivated by these factors serve G-d out of fear. They are not on the level of the prophets or the wise.

**RABBI MOSHE BEN MAIMON (MAIMONIDES, RAMBAM) 1135–1204**

Halachist, philosopher, author, and physician. Maimonides was born in Córdoba, Spain. After the conquest of Córdoba by the Almohads, he fled Spain and eventually settled in Cairo, Egypt. There, he became the leader of the Jewish community and served as court physician to the vizier of Egypt. He is most noted for authoring the *Mishneh Torah*, an encyclopedic arrangement of Jewish law; and for his philosophical work, *Guide for the Perplexed*. His rulings on Jewish law are integral to the formation of Halachic consensus.

## III. A DESIRE FOR A HOME

We've made the case that the world doesn't revolve around us: that we weren't created for our own sake, but for something greater—for G-d's glory. But that raises a pretty obvious question:

Why would G-d need that? What does G-d get out of creating a world? And why would He want us to serve Him?

***SHTETL* SYNAGOGUE WITH SHABBAT CLOUDS**
Mark Podwal (1945–2024), acrylic, gouache, and colored pencil on paper

TEXT 3

## G-d's Desire

Midrash, *Tanchuma,* Naso 16

בְּשָׁעָה שֶׁבָּרָא הַקָּדוֹשׁ בָּרוּךְ הוּא אֶת הָעוֹלָם, נִתְאַוָּה שֶׁיְּהֵא לוֹ דִירָה בַּתַּחְתּוֹנִים כְּמוֹ שֶׁיֵּשׁ בָּעֶלְיוֹנִים.

When G-d created the world, He desired to have a dwelling place in the lower realms just as He has in the upper realms.

***TANCHUMA***

A Midrashic work bearing the name of Rabbi Tanchuma, a 4th-century Talmudic sage quoted often in this work. "Midrash" is the designation of a particular genre of rabbinic literature usually forming a running commentary on specific books of the Bible. *Tanchuma* provides textual exegeses, expounds upon the biblical narrative, and develops and illustrates moral principles. *Tanchuma* is unique in that many of its sections commence with a Halachic discussion, which subsequently leads into non-Halachic teachings.

**SYNAGOGUE IN TARNÓW, POLAND**

Rafael Chwoles (Lithuanian/French, 1913–2002), oil on canvas, 1979

**TEXT 4**

## Purpose on the Lowest Level

Rabbi Shneur Zalman of Liadi, *Tanya, Likutei Amarim*, ch. 36

וְזֶהוּ עִנְיַן הִשְׁתַּלְשְׁלוּת הָעוֹלָמוֹת וִירִידָתָם מִמַּדְרֵגָה לְמַדְרֵגָה עַל יְדֵי רִיבּוּי הַלְבוּשִׁים הַמַּסְתִּירִים הָאוֹר וְהַחַיּוּת שֶׁמִּמֶּנּוּ יִתְבָּרֵךְ, עַד שֶׁנִּבְרָא עוֹלָם הַזֶּה הַגַּשְׁמִי וְהַחוּמְרִי מַמָּשׁ, וְהוּא הַתַּחְתּוֹן בְּמַדְרֵגָה שֶׁאֵין תַּחְתּוֹן לְמַטָּה מִמֶּנּוּ בְּעִנְיַן הֶסְתֵּר אוֹרוֹ יִתְבָּרֵךְ וְחֹשֶׁךְ כָּפוּל וּמְכוּפָּל, עַד שֶׁהוּא מָלֵא קְלִיפּוֹת וְסִטְרָא אָחֳרָא שֶׁהֵן נֶגֶד ה' מַמָּשׁ, לוֹמַר: "אֲנִי וְאַפְסִי עוֹד".

וְהִנֵּה, תַּכְלִית הִשְׁתַּלְשְׁלוּת הָעוֹלָמוֹת וִירִידָתָם מִמַּדְרֵגָה לְמַדְרֵגָה אֵינוֹ בִּשְׁבִיל עוֹלָמוֹת הָעֶלְיוֹנִים, הוֹאִיל וְלָהֶם יְרִידָה מֵאוֹר פָּנָיו יִתְבָּרֵךְ. אֶלָּא הַתַּכְלִית הוּא עוֹלָם הַזֶּה הַתַּחְתּוֹן. שֶׁכָּךְ עָלָה בִּרְצוֹנוֹ יִתְבָּרֵךְ, לִהְיוֹת נַחַת רוּחַ לְפָנָיו יִתְבָּרַךְ כַּד אִתְכַּפְיָא סִטְרָא אָחֳרָא וְאִתְהַפֵּךְ חֲשׁוֹכָא לִנְהוֹרָא, שֶׁיָּאִיר אוֹר ה' אֵין סוֹף בָּרוּךְ הוּא בִּמְקוֹם הַחֹשֶׁךְ וְהַסִּטְרָא אָחֳרָא שֶׁל כָּל עוֹלָם הַזֶּה כּוּלוֹ.

This is the idea behind the chain-like progression of the spiritual worlds—how they descend step-by-step, through many layers that act like coverings, hiding the light and life-force that come from G-d. Eventually, this process leads to the Creation of our physical, material world. This world is the lowest of all—it hides G-d's presence more than any other. It's a world of deep and layered darkness, filled with *kelipah* (spiritual coverings)

**RABBI SHNEUR ZALMAN OF LIADI (ALTER REBBE) 1745–1812**

Chasidic rebbe, Halachic authority, and founder of the Chabad movement. The Alter Rebbe was born in Liozna, Belarus, and was among the principal students of the Magid of Mezeritch. His numerous works include the *Tanya*, an early classic containing the fundamentals of Chabad Chasidism; and *Shulchan Aruch HaRav*, an expanded and reworked code of Jewish law.

and *sitra achara* (forces that oppose holiness), which can even deny G-d altogether, saying things like, "It's just me—nothing else matters."

This descent wasn't for the sake of the higher worlds. For them, each step down is a loss of closeness to G-d. The real purpose was this lowest world. This is what G-d wanted—that He would take pleasure when the *sitra achara* is overcome and darkness is turned into light, and that His infinite light should shine precisely here, in the very place where He seems most hidden.

TEXT 5

## *Mitzvah* Effects

Ibid., ch. 37

בַּעֲשִׂיָּיתָהּ מַמְשִׁיךְ הָאָדָם גִילוּי אוֹר אֵין סוֹף בָּרוּךְ הוּא מִלְמַעְלָה לְמַטָּה לְהִתְלַבֵּשׁ בְּגַשְׁמִיּוּת עוֹלָם הַזֶּה . . . שֶׁהֵם כָּל דְבָרִים הַטְהוֹרִים וּמוּתָּרִים שֶׁנַּעֲשֵׂית בָּהֶם הַמִּצְוָה מַעֲשִׂיית, כְּגוֹן: קְלַף הַתְּפִילִין וּמְזוּזָה וְסֵפֶר תּוֹרָה.

When we do a *mitzvah*—an act that G-d commanded—we draw His infinite light down into this physical world . . . into the actual, tangible objects we use to fulfill the *mitzvah*. For example, the parchment used to make *tefilin*, a *mezuzah*, or a Torah scroll.

## IV. IT'S IN THE DETAILS

We've explained that identifying with purpose means realizing that the purpose lies beyond ourselves—that our role is to serve G-d, do *mitzvot*, and create a home for Him in this world.

This shift also has another major implication: once we see life through the lens of Divine purpose, meaning starts to show up *everywhere*.

**JERUSALEM IN PRAYER**
David Rakia (Vienna, 1928–2012, Jerusalem), oil on canvas, Jerusalem, 1980s

TEXT 6

## Everything Serves

Talmud, Kidushin 82b

כּוּלָם לֹא נִבְרְאוּ אֶלָּא לְשַׁמְּשֵׁנִי, וַאֲנִי לֹא
נִבְרֵאתִי אֶלָּא לְשַׁמֵּשׁ אֶת קוֹנִי.

Everything was created only to serve me, and I was created only to serve my Creator.

TEXT 7

## "Created for a Purpose"

Talmud, Shabbat 77b

אָמַר רַב יְהוּדָה אָמַר רַב: כָּל מַה שֶׁבָּרָא הַקָדוֹשׁ
בָּרוּךְ הוּא בְּעוֹלָמוֹ, לֹא בָּרָא דָבָר אֶחָד לְבַטָלָה.

Rabbi Yehudah said in the name of Rav: "Everything that G-d created in His world, He created for a purpose—nothing was made without purpose."

**BABYLONIAN TALMUD**

A literary work of monumental proportions that draws upon the legal, spiritual, intellectual, ethical, and historical traditions of Judaism. The 37 tractates of the Babylonian Talmud contain the teachings of the Jewish sages from the period after the destruction of the 2nd Temple through the 5th century CE. It has served as the primary vehicle for the transmission of the Oral Law and the education of Jews over the centuries; it is the entry point for all subsequent legal, ethical, and theological Jewish scholarship.

**TEXT 8**

## Pure Wealth

Talmud, Zevachim 88b

אֵין עֲנִיּוּת בִּמְקוֹם עֲשִׁירוּת.

There is no place for poverty in a place of wealth.

**TEXT 9**

## The Leaders' Wagons

Numbers 7:2–3

וַיַּקְרִיבוּ נְשִׂיאֵי יִשְׂרָאֵל רָאשֵׁי בֵּית אֲבֹתָם, הֵם
נְשִׂיאֵי הַמַּטֹּת הֵם הָעֹמְדִים עַל הַפְּקֻדִים.

וַיָּבִיאוּ אֶת קָרְבָּנָם לִפְנֵי ה': שֵׁשׁ עֶגְלֹת צָב
וּשְׁנֵי עָשָׂר בָּקָר, עֲגָלָה עַל שְׁנֵי הַנְּשִׂאִים וְשׁוֹר
לְאֶחָד, וַיַּקְרִיבוּ אוֹתָם לִפְנֵי הַמִּשְׁכָּן.

The leaders of Israel, the heads of the families—they were the leaders of the tribes, the ones who stood over the census—presented [their offerings].

They brought their offering before G-d: six covered wagons and twelve oxen, a wagon for every two leaders and an ox for each one. They brought them before the Tabernacle.

TEXT 10

## Maximizing Utility

The Rebbe, Rabbi Menachem Mendel Schneerson,
*Likutei Sichot* 28, pp. 47–48

כָּאטְשׁ דִי הַנְהָגָה אִין דֶעם מִקְדָשׁ אִיז בְּאוֹפֶן פוּן עֲשִׁירוּת, אִיז דָאס אָבֶּער נִיט אִין אַן אוֹפֶן פוּן לְבַטָלָה, חַס וְשָׁלוֹם. נַאָר עֶס אִיז נִיכָּר וִוי יֶעדֶער פְּרָט פִּירְט דוּרְךְ זַיין תַּפְקִיד וְתַכְלִית בְּרִיאָתוֹ.

אוּן דֶערִיבֶּער, וִויבַּאלְד אַז אוֹיף לָשֵׂאת אֶת הַמִשְׁכָּן אִיז גֶענוּג י"ב בָּקָר אוּן שֵׁשׁ עֲגָלוֹת (בְּאוֹרֶךְ וְרוֹחַב מְסוּיָים) הָאט קֵיין אָרְט נִיט אַז מֶען זָאל דֶערוֹיף מוֹסִיף זַיין. אוּן דֶעם וְהוֹתֵר וָואס אִיז דָא, דַארְף (אוּן מוּז) עֶר אוֹיסְנוּצְן אִין אַ צְוֵויטְן עִנְיָן בַּמִשְׁכָּן.

Although the service in the Temple was carried out with richness and grandeur, there was never any waste—G-d forbid. It was clear that every detail served a specific function and fulfilled the unique purpose for which it was made.

That's why, if twelve oxen and six wagons (of a specific length and width) were enough to transport the Tabernacle, there was no need to bring more. Any surplus materials had to be directed toward another need within the Tabernacle.

**RABBI MENACHEM MENDEL SCHNEERSON 1902–1994**

The towering Jewish leader of the 20th century, known as "the Lubavitcher Rebbe," or simply as "the Rebbe." Born in southern Ukraine, the Rebbe escaped Nazi-occupied Europe, arriving in the U.S. in June 1941. The Rebbe inspired and guided the revival of traditional Judaism after the European devastation, impacting virtually every Jewish community the world over. The Rebbe often emphasized that the performance of just one additional good deed could usher in the era of Mashiach. The Rebbe's scholarly talks and writings have been printed in more than 200 volumes.

**TEXT 11**

## Calming Purpose

The Rebbe, Rabbi Menachem Mendel Schneerson,
*Sefer Hasichot* 5751:2, p. 553

בְּפַשְׁטוּת הַדְבָרִים, בְּטֶבַע בְּנֵי אָדָם: בִּשְׁעַת אַ מֶענְטְשׁ פִּילְט נִיט דִי כַּוָונָה וְתַכְלִית אִין זַיין לֶעבְּן (אַז "אֲנִי נִבְרֵאתִי לְשַׁמֵשׁ אֶת קוֹנִי"), קֶען עֶר נִיט שְׁטֵיין מִיט אַן אֱמֶת'ע מְנוּחָה וְהִתְיַישְׁבוּת, וָוארוּם דִי שִׁינוּיֵי הַזְמַן וְהַמָקוֹם אוּן אַלֶע רִיבּוּי פְּרָטִים וּפְרָטֵי פְּרָטִים פוּן זַיין לֶעבְּן זַיינֶען גוֹרֵם אַ שְׁטֶענְדִיקֶע אוּמְרוּ, וָואס "שְׁפַּאלְט" אִים פַאנַאנְדֶער;

דַוְקָא בִּשְׁעַת עֶר דֶערְהֶערְט דִי צִיל - דִי כַּוָונָה וְתַכְלִית - וָואס לִיגְט בְּתוֹךְ דִי אַלֶע פְּרָטִים, דֶעמוֹלְט בְּרֶענְגְט עֶס אִים אַ מְנוּחָה, וָואס אִיז הֶעכֶער פַאר דֶער תְּנוּעָה וְשִׁינוּי פוּן פְּרָטֵי הַחַיִים, אוּן בְּמֵילָא - צוּ שְׁלֵימוּת הָאָדָם, וִוי מְ'זֶעט בְּפַשְׁטוּת אַז אַ מֶענְטְשׁ שְׁטֵייט מֶער בִּשְׁלֵימוּת וֶוען עֶר הָאט מְנוּחָה, מְנוּחַת הַנֶפֶשׁ וּמְנוּחַת הַגוּף.

It is basic human nature that when a person doesn't feel the purpose and goal of their life—that "I was created only to serve my Creator"—they cannot experience real inner calm or peace of mind. That's because the constant changes in time and place, along with the endless details and sub-details of life, create ongoing tension and instability that fragment the person.

But when a person becomes aware of the goal—the purpose and meaning—behind all those details, it brings a deep sense of calm. That calm transcends the movement and fluctuation of life's particulars, and it leads a person toward wholeness. It's obvious that a person functions with greater integrity and balance when they have such peace—both peace of mind and peace of body.

TEXT 12A

## The Seventh Day

Genesis 2:1–2

וַיְכֻלּוּ הַשָּׁמַיִם וְהָאָרֶץ וְכָל צְבָאָם. וַיְכַל אֱלֹקִים
בַּיּוֹם הַשְּׁבִיעִי מְלַאכְתּוֹ אֲשֶׁר עָשָׂה, וַיִּשְׁבֹּת
בַּיּוֹם הַשְּׁבִיעִי מִכָּל מְלַאכְתּוֹ אֲשֶׁר עָשָׂה.

The heavens and the earth and all they contain were completed. On the seventh day, G-d completed the work He had done and rested from all His labor.

TEXT 12B

## Completed by Rest

Rashi, Genesis 2:2

מֶה הָיָה הָעוֹלָם חָסֵר? מְנוּחָה, בָּאת שַׁבָּת בָּאת מְנוּחָה - כָּלְתָה וְנִגְמְרָה הַמְּלָאכָה.

What was the world lacking? Rest. The Shabbat came, and with it came rest. With that, the work was completed and finished.

**RABBI SHLOMO YITZCHAKI (RASHI) 1040–1105**

Most noted biblical and Talmudic commentator. Born in Troyes, France, Rashi studied in the famed *yeshivot* of Mainz and Worms. His commentaries on the Pentateuch and the Talmud, which focus on the straightforward meaning of the text, appear in virtually every edition of the Talmud and Bible.

TEXT 13

## The Rest of Purpose

The Rebbe, Rabbi Menachem Mendel Schneerson, *Sefer Hasichot* 5751:2, p. 552

יוֹם הַשַּׁבָּת הָאט אַרײַנְגֶעבְּרַאכְט מְנוּחָה אִין עוֹלָם ("בָּאת שַׁבָּת בָּאת מְנוּחָה"), וָוארוּם דִי בְּרִיאָה אִיז פַארְעֶנְדִיקְט גֶעוָוארְן בְּשֵׁשֶׁת יְמֵי בְּרֵאשִׁית, "וַיְכוּלוּ הַשָּׁמַיִם וְהָאָרֶץ וְכָל צְבָאָם, וַיְכַל אֱלֹקִים גו׳ מְלַאכְתּוֹ אֲשֶׁר עָשָׂה", אוּן עֶס הָאט זִיךְ אָנְגֶעהֶערְט בְּכָל הָעוֹלָם וּבְכָל פְּרָטֵי הָעוֹלָם - אִין אַלֶע שִׁינוּיִים וְחִילוּקֵי דַרְגוֹת פוּן זְמַן וּמָקוֹם - וִוי דָאס אַלְץ אִיז בַּאשַׁאפְן גֶעוָוארְן פוּן ה׳ **אֶחָד**, דִי כַּוָונָה **אַחַת** פוּן דֶעם אוֹיבֶּערְשְׁטְן בְּכָל פְּרָטֵי הַבְּרִיאָה, וָואס דָאס אִיז הֶעכֶער פַאר דִי שִׁינוּיֵי הַזְמַן וְהַמָּקוֹם, אוּן דֶעריבֶּער בְּרֶענְגְט עֶס אַרײַן **מְנוּחָה** אִין כָּל הַבְּרִיאָה.

Shabbat brought rest into the world—"The Shabbat came, and with it came rest"—because with the completion of Creation during the six days ("The heavens and the earth and all they contain were completed. On the seventh day, G-d completed the work He had done and rested from all His labor."), something shifted. At that point, it became apparent throughout the world, in every detail and across all variations of time and space, that everything was created by the *one* G-d, and that a *single unified* purpose runs through all of Creation. That purpose is beyond the changes of time and place—and it's what brings true peace and tranquility to the entire world.

FIGURE 3.1

## Six Days of Creation and Shabbat

| WEEKDAY | SHABBAT |
|---|---|
| Action | Rest |
| Fragmentation | Unity |
| Process | Purpose |
| Change | Centering |

## V. TALENTS AND SKILLS

The idea we've been exploring isn't just about giving meaning to different parts of our schedule—work, study, downtime. It goes deeper than that. It extends to every part of who we are. A life of true meaning is one in which *nothing* is left out—not even the most personal, individual aspects of ourselves. In a meaningful life, no part of us is empty or random. Everything can—and must—be directed toward our purpose.

**THE CHAZZAN'S PRAYER (DETAIL)**
Abraham Jacobi Bogdanove (Minsk, Russia, 1888–1946, New York), oil on masonite

TEXT 14

## Honor with Your Skills

Midrash, *Yalkut Shimoni*, I Kings, section 221

כְּתִיב, "כַּבֵּד אֶת ה' מֵהוֹנֶךָ" (מִשְׁלֵי ג, ט), מִמָּה שֶׁחֲנָנְךָ. שֶׁאִם הָיָה קוֹלְךָ נָאֶה, עֲבוֹר לִפְנֵי הַתֵּיבָה. חִיָּיא בֶּן אֲחוֹתוֹ שֶׁל רַבִּי אֶלְעָזָר הַקַּפָּר הָיָה קוֹלוֹ נָאֶה, וְהָיָה אוֹמֵר לוֹ, "חִיָּיא בְּנִי! עֲמוֹד וְכַבֵּד אֶת ה' מִמָּה שֶׁחֲנָנְךָ".

The Torah states, "Honor G-d with your possessions" (PROVERBS 3:9)—with the skills He graced you with. If you have a beautiful voice, lead the congregation in prayer.

**YALKUT SHIMONI**

A Midrash that covers the entire biblical text. Its material is collected from all over rabbinic literature, including the Babylonian and Jerusalem Talmuds and various ancient Midrashic texts. It contains several passages from *Midrashim* that have been lost, as well as different versions of existing *Midrashim*. It is unclear when and by whom this Midrash was redacted.

TEXT 15

## Purposeful Talents

The Rebbe, Rabbi Menachem Mendel Schneerson, *Likutei Sichot* 28, p. 47

פוּן דֶעם אִיז דִי הוֹרָאָה צוּ יֶעדְן אִידְן . . . אוֹיף וִויפְל עֶר דַארְף זַיין נִזְהָר אַז יֶעדֶער כֹּחַ וּבְכָל פְּרָטָיו וָואס דֶער אוֹיבֶּערְשְׁטֶער הָאט אִים גֶעגֶעבְּן זָאל נִיט זַיין לְבַטָּלָה חַס וְשָׁלוֹם.

נָאר אוֹיסְנוּצְן אִים אִין דֶער פוּלְסְטֶער מָאס פַאר דֶעם תַּכְלִית וְתַפְקִיד צוּלִיבּ וֶועלְכְן דֶער אוֹיבֶּערְשְׁטֶער הָאט אִים בַּאשַׁאפְן - "אֲנִי נִבְרֵאתִי לְשַׁמֵּשׁ אֶת קוֹנִי".

This is a lesson for every Jew: we must be careful to ensure that every ability G-d has given us—even the smallest detail—is never wasted, G-d forbid.

Instead, each one should be used to its fullest extent for the purpose and mission for which G-d created us: "I was created only to serve my Creator."

**EXERCISE 3.2**

**What's something I do regularly that I've never thought of as meaningful? Could it be?**

**What's a skill I've underappreciated in myself that might actually be part of my mission?**

## VI. CONCLUSION

TEXT 16

### The Cost of Fulfillment

Rabbi Lazer Gurkow, *Mission Possible: Living with Higher Purpose*, p. 12

A man once called out to G-d and asked for fulfillment. G-d appeared and said, "As it happens, I have some fulfillment available today at a reasonable price. How much have you got in your pocket?"

"Twenty dollars."

"Well, as it happens, I'm running a special. The cost of fulfillment today is twenty dollars."

"But that's all I have, and if I give it to you, I won't be able to buy gas for my car."

"Ah," says G-d, "you have a car. The price for fulfillment just went up. Twenty dollars plus your car."

"But without my car, how will I get to my job?"

"Ah, you have a job; the price for fulfillment went up again. Twenty dollars, plus your car and your job."

"But without a job, how will I provide for my family?"

**RABBI LAZER GURKOW**

Author and lecturer. Rabbi Gurkow is the spiritual leader of Congregation Beth Tefilah in London, Ontario. He lectures extensively on a variety of Jewish topics, and his articles appear in many print and online publications. Rabbi Gurkow is a member of the Rohr Jewish Learning Institute (JLI) curriculum team, and he authored *Portraits in Leadership*, a highly popular JLI course.

"Ah, you have a family? The price for fulfillment will include your family too. Do we have a deal?"

The man decides to keep quiet this time and he agrees.

"But one more thing," says G-d. "Before I give you fulfillment, I want to give you these twenty dollars, but it is not your money; it is mine. I want you to be my agent and spend it as I would. I also want you to take the car, but remember, it isn't your car, it is mine, and I want you to drive it to the places that I would. I also want you to take the job, but it's my job that you have, so I want you to behave there as I would. Finally, I want you to take the family, but it's not your family; it's mine. Care for them as I would."

And with this, the man finally found fulfillment.

## KEY POINTS

1. G-d created our world because He desired a home in the lowest, most resistant place, where His presence is hidden and belief isn't automatic. G-d wants us, with our free will and limited perception, to choose to make this world into a home for Him.

2. Every *mitzvah* act makes a piece of the world into a home for G-d, advancing the purpose for which the universe was created.

3. When we succeed in playing our role in G-d's grand cosmic story, our every action and moment is imbued with cosmic significance, and our lives become meaningful.

4. Everything within the world fits into the Divine plan; nothing is random. Even mundane, non-"religious"-looking activities can be part of the Divine purpose of Creation when we perform them with the intention of helping us serve G-d better.

5 Our talents are meant to be part of our Divine mission. G-d gave us the specific skill set we have because there's something only we can contribute to His world. When we direct those strengths toward our purpose, the ordinary becomes sacred, and our lives become meaningful.

6 Living with the awareness that every part of reality has a role and a place in G-d's plan brings unity and harmony to every element of our lives, infusing us with a feeling of fulfillment and tranquility.

## Maximum Utility

This spread presents two biblical examples illustrating the principle of maximizing every inch of potential.

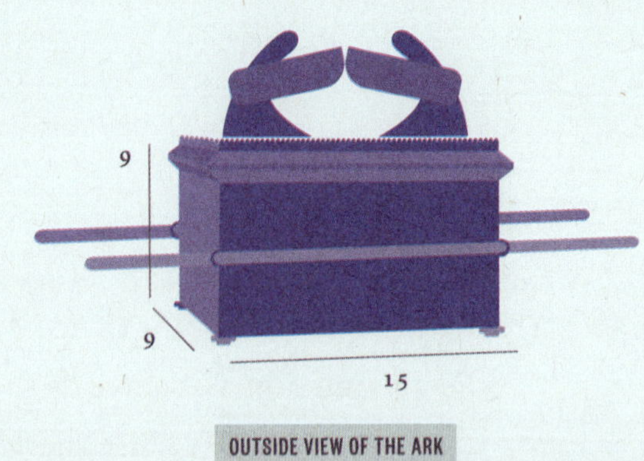


OUTSIDE VIEW OF THE ARK

### Inside the Ark

The Ark in the Holy Temple held the tablets given to Moses at Mount Sinai: both the shards of the first set that was broken, as well as the complete second set. According to one opinion in the Talmud, the master copy of the Torah, written by Moses himself, was also stored within the Ark. This Torah scroll was used at certain public readings conducted by the king and high priest.

The Talmud and Midrashim record a few different opinions about how the tablets were arranged inside the Ark. All opinions agree that the entire space of length and width of the Ark was utilized, but they differ on exactly how this was accomplished. The illustration here follows Rabbi Meir, the first opinion cited in the Talmud, Bava Batra 14a–b.

All measurements are given in *tefachim* (handbreadths), a traditional unit of length. One *tefach* equals 3.15 inches.

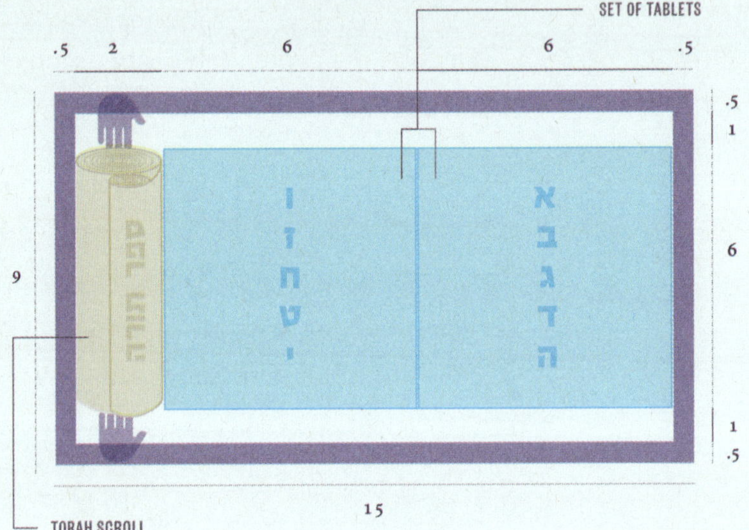


The *tefach*-wide empty space on either side was designed to allow for the scroll to be removed and replaced.

AERIAL VIEW OF THE ARK'S CONTENTS

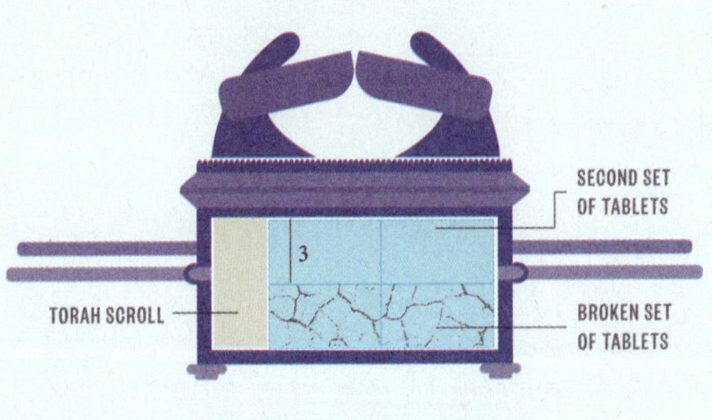


SIDE VIEW OF THE ARK'S CONTENTS

## Stacking the Wagons

The Torah relates (Numbers 1:3) that the twelve princes of the tribes of Israel contributed six wagons, each drawn by two oxen, for the purpose of transporting the Tabernacle during the Israelites' journeys in the desert.

The components of the Tabernacle were divided into two for the purposes of transportation. The Levite family of Merari was responsible for transporting the beams that formed the framework of the Tabernacle, while the family of Gershon was responsible for transporting the curtains and animal hides that covered the structure. With Merari having the larger load to carry, they were given four of the wagons, and Gershon received two (Numbers 1:7–8).

The Talmud (Shabbat 98a–99a) presents a detailed logistical discussion of how the 48 beams were loaded onto the four wagons of the Merari family, 12 beams on each wagon. Following is a visual representation of the Talmud's conclusion.

All measurements are given in *amot* (cubits), a traditional unit of length. One *amah* equals 18.9 inches.

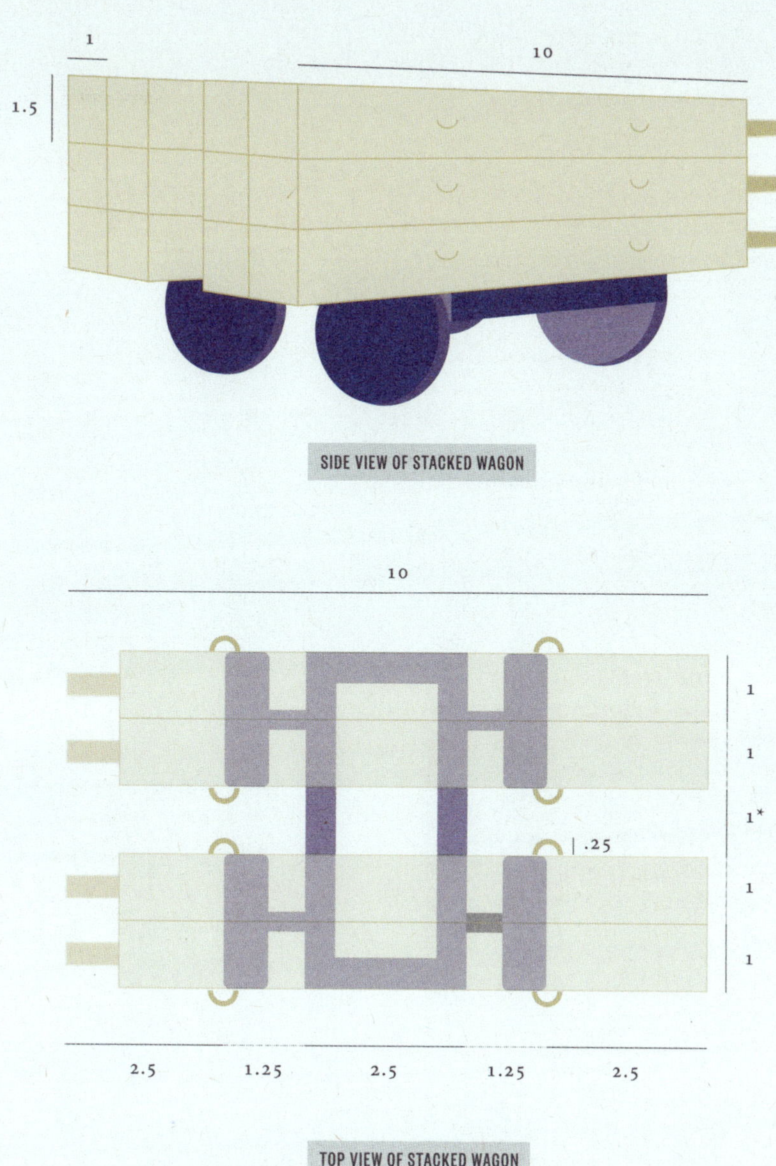


SIDE VIEW OF STACKED WAGON

TOP VIEW OF STACKED WAGON

* The wagons were 5 *amot* in length in order to allow for the beams to be stacked alternatively, in 3 piles on their 1.5 *amah*-wide sides, if the movers found this arrangement preferable. A minimum of a half-amah of extra space was required for stability.

## Psychology References

Martela, F., & Steger, M. F. (2016). The three meanings of meaning in life: Distinguishing coherence, purpose, and significance. *The Journal of Positive Psychology*, 11(5), 531–545.

Kim, E. S., et al. (2022). Sense of purpose in life and subsequent physical, behavioral, and psychosocial health: An outcome-wide approach. *American Journal of Health Promotion*, 36(1), 137–147.

Chen, Y., et al. (2019). Sense of mission and subsequent health and well-being among young adults: An outcome-wide analysis. *American Journal of Epidemiology*, 188(4), 664–673.

Juan, X., et al. (2021). Inner peace as a contribution to human flourishing in measuring well-being. In *Measuring Well-Being: Interdisciplinary Perspectives from the Social Sciences and the Humanities*, Oxford University Press, New York, N.Y.

Yuliawati, L., et al. (2025). Who I am and who I want to be: The positive effect of self-concept clarity on purpose, life satisfaction, and personal meaning among Chinese and Indonesian emerging adults. *Current Issues in Personality Psychology*, 13(1), 50–57.

Xiang, G., et al. (2023). Self-concept clarity and subjective well-being: Disentangling within- and between-person associations. *Journal of Happiness Studies,* 24(4), 1439–1461.

# LESSON 4

## MEANING IN THE RHYTHMS OF TIME

*As time flies by, is it just more of the same? Discover the rich texture of Jewish time, and how attuning ourselves to each moment's message enables profound spiritual purpose.*

**"KAREV YOM" (THE MYSTICAL MOMENT OF EVERY DAY) (DETAIL)**
Berit Engen, woven tapestry, linen yarn, Oak Park, Illinois, 2009

## I. LIVING TIMEFULLY

In our previous three classes, we have been challenged by Jewish tradition to find meaning and purpose in our lives.

We've explored how meaning is something we cultivate. We create it through our focus, through our actions, and through our alignment with the values and purpose that the Torah lays out for us. We've seen how a life of meaning is something we build day by day through intentional behavior. That's a powerful idea. But if we stop there, something important is still missing.

Because even the most purposeful life can begin to feel mechanical. Get up, do the right things, go to bed, repeat. If meaning is just a matter of doing what's right again and again, how do we keep it fresh? How do we stop it from becoming rote?

**WHAT COMES NEXT COMES NEXT**
Joshua Meyer, oil on board, Cambridge, Massachusetts, 2012

## II. THE TEXTURE OF TIME

To dig into this topic, we need to begin by understanding something distinctive—perhaps even surprising—about the way Jewish tradition thinks about special days.

**BLOWING THE SHOFAR**
Seymour Rosenthal, watercolor on paper, New York, 1963

**EXERCISE 4.1A**

**Imagine you're walking with a child in Massachusetts and you come across a sign that reads, "Plymouth Rock, Landing Place of the Pilgrims, 1620." The child turns to you and asks, "Why did the *Mayflower* land *here*, of all places?" What would you say?**

**Now imagine you're walking with the same child in California and come upon a sign that says, "Welcome to Historic Mount Wilson Observatory." This time, the child asks, "Why did they build the observatory *here*?" How would you answer?**

**EXERCISE 4.1B**

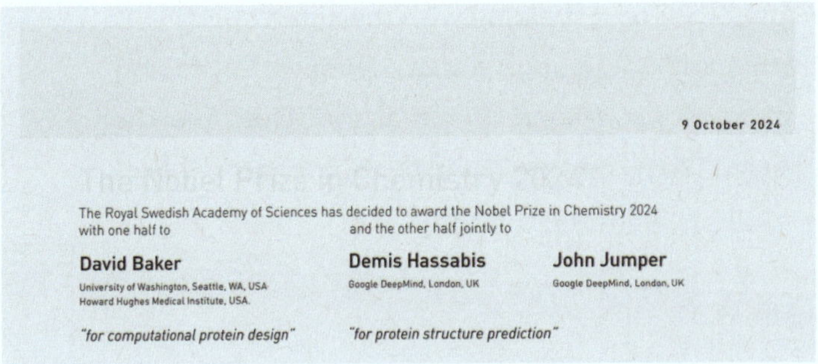

9 October 2024

The Royal Swedish Academy of Sciences has decided to award the Nobel Prize in Chemistry 2024 with one half to

**David Baker**
University of Washington, Seattle, WA, USA
Howard Hughes Medical Institute, USA

*"for computational protein design"*

and the other half jointly to

**Demis Hassabis**
Google DeepMind, London, UK

**John Jumper**
Google DeepMind, London, UK

*"for protein structure prediction"*

**Imagine you read in the newspaper that Dr. David Baker has been awarded the Nobel Prize in chemistry. You also read that Ivy, a Washington, D.C. resident, received a free Metrorail card and a $500 gift card for being the one-millionth passenger at Dulles Airport. If a child asked you why Dr. Baker got the Nobel Prize, what would you say?**

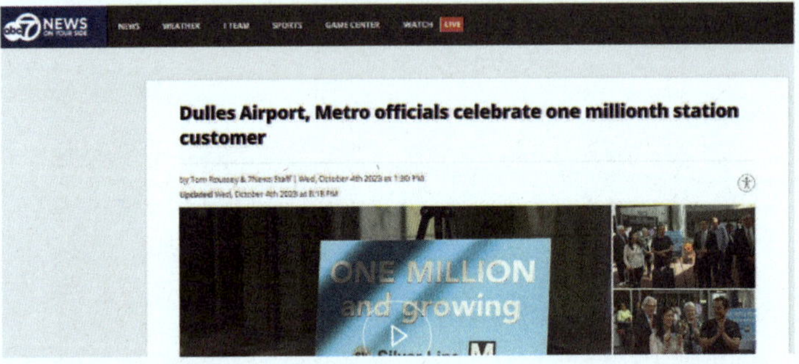

7NEWS ON YOUR SIDE | NEWS | WEATHER | I TEAM | SPORTS | GAME CENTER | WATCH | LIVE

**Dulles Airport, Metro officials celebrate one millionth station customer**

by Tom Roussey & 7News Staff | Wed, October 4th 2023 at 1:30 PM
Updated Wed, October 4th 2023 at 8:18 PM



**And if they asked why Ivy received the prize at the airport, how would you respond?**

**TEXT 1**

## The Shabbat Spice

Talmud, Shabbat 119b

אָמַר לוֹ קֵיסָר לְרַבִּי יְהוֹשֻׁעַ בֶּן חֲנַנְיָא: מִפְּנֵי מָה תַּבְשִׁיל שֶׁל שַׁבָּת רֵיחוֹ נוֹדֵף?

אָמַר לוֹ: תַּבְלִין אֶחָד יֵשׁ לָנוּ וְשַׁבָּת שְׁמוֹ, שֶׁאָנוּ מְטִילִין לְתוֹכוֹ וְרֵיחוֹ נוֹדֵף.

The Roman emperor asked Rabbi Yehoshua ben Chananya: "Why do the dishes of Shabbat produce such an enticing aroma?"

He answered, "We have a special spice, and it is called Shabbat. We place it in the Shabbat dishes, and it gives off a fragrant aroma."

**BABYLONIAN TALMUD**

A literary work of monumental proportions that draws upon the legal, spiritual, intellectual, ethical, and historical traditions of Judaism. The 37 tractates of the Babylonian Talmud contain the teachings of the Jewish sages from the period after the destruction of the 2nd Temple through the 5th century CE. It has served as the primary vehicle for the transmission of the Oral Law and the education of Jews over the centuries; it is the entry point for all subsequent legal, ethical, and theological Jewish scholarship.

***LA BÉNÉDICTION DE L'AÏEUL* (THE GRANDFATHER'S BLESSING)**
Edouard Moyse (Nancy, France, 1827–1908, Paris), oil on canvas

TEXT 2

## Yom Kippur Melody

"The Captain's Kol Nidrei," song written by Yom Tov Ehrlich and recorded on his *T'shuvah* album, 1962. Translation by Rabbi Eliyahu Friedman, for Avraham Fried's *Yiddish Gems* English album, 2010

He weaves through the streets, hot on the trail,
The melody stronger and stronger.
What is its message, what is its tale?
His heart can't hold out much longer. . . .

He spots a babushka, walking along,
Crossing a street in the middle.
Can she decipher the mysterious song,
Can she solve this great riddle?

"Grandma," he says, "please listen to me.
This song in my ear is quite bruising.
The melody is haunting. It won't let me be.
I fear that my mind I am losing."

"Your face tells me," comes the reply,
"That you are a Jew, my dear skipper.
You're churning, you're burning. I'll tell you why:
Tonight is the night of Yom Kippur."

**RABBI YOM TOV EHRLICH 1914–1990**

Composer and lyricist. Born in Kazhan-Haradok, Belarus, to a family of Stoliner Chasidim, Rabbi Ehrlich survived the war in Samarkand, Uzbekistan, and then moved to Williamsburg, in Brooklyn, New York. He produced over thirty records of his original Yiddish lyrics set to classic folk melodies. Classics in the Chasidic community, Rabbi Ehrlich's songs draw on the Jewish festivals, Chasidic stories, and his personal life experiences, conveying messages about Jewish values and faith.

**TEXT 3**

## Yom Kippur Mystery

Rabbi Shlomo Schwartz (Schwartzie) and Rabbi Mendel Schwartz, *I Love When That Happens* (Los Angeles: The Chai Center, 2019), pp. 85–86

The doctor told me that an average of five people per day [experience breakdowns] and are brought to NPI; few of them are Jewish. But, he said, "I have noticed that every single year, around the Jewish holidays, the Jewish admittance goes up dramatically. And on one day each year, admittance spikes closer to 20 people, with 15 of them Jewish."

"Which day is that?" I asked.

The doctor said, "Yom Kippur."

And here is the punchline: Each year, when admittance to NPI went up on Yom Kippur, it was on the Hebrew calendar date, the tenth day of Tishrei, not a consistent date on the secular calendar. The Jews who were brought in on Yom Kippur didn't even know it was Yom Kippur.

**RABBI SHLOMO SCHWARTZ 1945–2017**

Rabbi and speaker. Born in Atlantic City, New Jersey, Shlomo Schwartz (Schwartzie) joined Chabad as a teenager and studied at the Rabbinical College of America in Morristown, New Jersey. He founded the Chai Center in Los Angeles, and was known for his colorful and unconventional methods of engaging unaffiliated Jews.

TEXT 4

## Holy Time

Rabbi Mendel Kalmenson and Rabbi Zalman Abraham, *People of the Word* (Brooklyn, N.Y.: Chabad.org and Ezra Press, 2022), p. 346

Abraham wasn't celebrating an event in the future; he was tapping into a spiritual energy of freedom that was, and always is, present at that time of year. The energy of liberation is encoded into the composition of the annual cycle.

**RABBI MENDEL KALMENSON**

Author, lecturer, and noted expert on Chasidic thought. Rabbi Kalmenson serves as the rabbi of Beit Baruch and directs Chabad of Belgravia in Central London. He is the author of the popular titles *Positivity Bias* and *A Time to Heal*.

**RABBI ZALMAN ABRAHAM**

Author. Born in South Africa, Rabbi Zalman Abraham lives in Brooklyn, New York, and serves as director of The Wellness Institute—a division of the Rohr Jewish Learning Institute (JLI) dedicated to youth mental health. He is the coauthor of *People of the Word: Fifty Words That Shaped Jewish Thinking*.

TEXT 5

## Consequences of Violation

Rabbi Shneur Zalman of Liadi, *Tanya, Likutei Amarim*, ch. 46

לְפִי שֶׁאַף בְּנֶפֶשׁ בּוּר וְעַם הָאָרֶץ גָמוּר מֵאִיר אוֹר קְדֻשַּׁת שַׁבָּת וְיוֹם טוֹב . . . פּוֹגֵם בַּקְדֻשָּׁה שֶׁעַל נַפְשׁוֹ, כְּמוֹ בִּקְדֻשַּׁת נֶפֶשׁ הַצַּדִּיק.

For even a complete ignoramus or peasant is suffused with the light of the holiness of Shabbat and holidays. . . . [Any violation] blemishes the holiness that suffuses their soul, just as it would the holiness of the soul of a *tzadik*.

**RABBI SHNEUR ZALMAN OF LIADI (ALTER REBBE) 1745–1812**

Chasidic rebbe, Halachic authority, and founder of the Chabad movement. The Alter Rebbe was born in Liozna, Belarus, and was among the principal students of the Magid of Mezeritch. His numerous works include the *Tanya*, an early classic containing the fundamentals of Chabad Chasidism; and *Shulchan Aruch HaRav*, an expanded and reworked code of Jewish law.

## III. EXTRACTING MEANING FROM THE CHANGING TIMES

Time is not a flat, uniform surface. It's textured—peaks, valleys, turning points—each moment carrying a unique spiritual quality. Just as certain terrains are better suited to particular activities (you plant grapes in Napa Valley, not Nebraska), certain times are more conducive to specific forms of spiritual growth. By aligning our efforts with the distinctive energy of each moment—whether it's a day of the week, a season, or a festival—we're better equipped to thrive in our spiritual lives.

**MASHIACH TIME TRAIN**
Haim Borosh, oil on canvas, Israel

TEXT 6

## Wells in Time

Rabbi Yanki Tauber, *Inside Time* (Brooklyn, N.Y.: Meaningful Life Center, 2015), vol. 1, pp. 40–41

Each festival marks a point in our journey through time at which our Heavenly Father . . . supplied us with the resources that nurture our spiritual lives. On Passover, we were granted the gift of freedom; on Shavuot, G-d . . . gave us His Torah . . . our charter as His kingdom of priests and a holy people; Rosh Hashanah is the day on which G-d first became King; on Yom Kippur, G-d . . . grant[ed] us the gift of *teshuvah*—the capacity to rectify and transform a deficient past; . . . Chanukah marks the salvation of the Jewish soul—the triumph of light and purity over darkness and adulteration; the miracle of Purim, the salvation of the Jewish body . . . and so with all the festivals and special dates and periods on our calendar.

**RABBI YANKI TAUBER 1965–**

Chasidic scholar and author. A native of Brooklyn, N.Y., Rabbi Tauber is an internationally renowned author who specializes in adapting the teachings of the Lubavitcher Rebbe. He is the editor of *The Book of Jewish Knowledge* and has written numerous articles and books including *Once Upon a Chassid* and *Beyond the Letter of the Law*. He has also authored several bestselling JLI courses.

EXERCISE 4.2

**Here is a table of central Chanukah themes. Choose one and consider how it might enhance your own Jewish practice, by doing something new or by reenergizing something you already do. How might the message of Chanukah infuse your regular year-round observance with deeper purpose?**

| | CHANUKAH ENERGY | APPLICATION TO LIFE |
|---|---|---|
| **ALWAYS GO UP** | Each night of Chanukah, we add a new candle, building light and never remaining the same. | Jewish life, too, must grow. Stagnation is not an option for a living soul. |
| **SELF-SACRIFICE** | The Maccabees fought against impossible odds, risking everything for what they believed in. | There are moments when we, too, must stand for truth—even when it costs us. |
| **DO YOUR BEST** | The Maccabees could have settled for impure oil, but they insisted on doing the *mitzvah* in the most beautiful, uncompromised way. | When we strive for excellence in our *mitzvah* observance, G-d meets us halfway—with miracles. |
| **THE LAST JUG OF OIL** | One small, sealed jug—untouched, undefiled—held the key to the miracle. | Every Jew has a pure inner core that can never be contaminated. When we connect to that essence, transformation begins. |
| **LIGHTING UP DARKNESS** | Chanukah candles are lit specifically after nightfall. The *mitzvah* isn't to light in broad daylight—but to bring light where it's cold and dark. | Torah can illuminate even the hardest moments of life. |
| **OUTDOOR JUDAISM** | The Chanukah lights are meant to shine outward, onto the street. | Judaism isn't just a private practice—it's something we're meant to share, to live publicly and proudly. |

**Feel free to write your reflection below. How can one of these themes help you bring more intention, courage, or light into your current Jewish practice?**

# The Jewish Map of Time

## *Days of the Week*

Every day of the week is associated with a specific *sefirah*—a Divine attribute. Chasidic teachings explain the implications for the Divine service of the day.

| DAY | *SEFIRAH* | SERVICE OF THE DAY |
|---|---|---|
| **SUNDAY** | *CHESED* KINDNESS | Love: Love for G-d, our fellows, and all that is good and holy; a desire to connect to G-d and enjoy a relationship with Him through emulating His kind and gracious ways |
| **MONDAY** | *GEVURAH* STRENGTH | Awe and reverence: Reverence for G-d, along with a general appreciation for boundaries and a commitment to maintaining dignified and sanctified behavior; a desire to see justice prevail and wrongdoers held accountable |
| **TUESDAY** | *TIFERET* BEAUTY | Focus on beauty and harmony: Appreciating G-d's glory and the harmony of His Divine attributes; a resolve not just to serve G-d, but to do so with grace, refinement, and beauty |
| **WEDNESDAY** | *NETZACH* VICTORY | Perseverance: Determination to overcome one's undesirable character traits and habits; a steadfast commitment to advancing G-d's purpose in the world, no matter the obstacles or resistance |
| **THURSDAY** | *HOD* SPLENDOR | Recognizing G-d's splendor by focusing on the greatness of His creations. This leads one to humility and gratitude and praise of G-d. |
| **FRIDAY** | *YESOD* FOUNDATION | The foundational power of connection and relationships—especially the connection with G-d, marked by genuine pleasure and heartfelt passion |
| **SHABBOS** | *MALCHUT* ROYALTY | Withdrawal from creative activity to focus on G-d and accept His sovereignty |

Sources: Rabbi Shalom Dovber Schneersohn, *Kuntres Umaayan* 19:2; Rabbi Shneur Zalman of Liadi, *Tanya*, *Igeret Hakodesh* 15

## *Days of the Month*

The moon symbolizes the Jewish people, and the sun represents G-d. This chart presents the Rebbe's explanation of how the dynamics of the moon-sun relationship over the course of the Jewish calendar month should be reflected in our Divine service.

| DAY/S | MOON PHASE | SPIRITUAL SIGNIFICANCE |
|---|---|---|
| DAY 1 | NEW MOON  | The moon symbolizes the Jewish people, and the sun represents G-d. G-d is the all-powerful and unchanging Source of light, and the Jewish people are the waxing and waning recipients of His light. The birth of the new moon represents a renewed union between G-d and the Jewish people. |
| DAYS 2–14 | WAXING MOON  | The waxing of the moon reflects our need to continually grow in our service of G-d, building upon each day's progress and never remaining stagnant. |
| DAY 15 | FULL MOON  | The full moon represents the peak of our spiritual achievements. |
| DAYS 16–29* | WANING MOON  | Our great achievements, which culminated on the fifteenth of the month, can lead us to feelings of pride and haughtiness. In the second half of the month, our focus shifts to cultivating *bitul*—removing our sense of self from the picture so that we should only feel G-d and His will. |
| DAY 30* | DISAPPEARING MOON  | After removing any sense of self, the moon's light is no longer visible: it is fully aligned with the sun—G-d. This sets us up for the renewed union of the following day: the first of the new month. |

*Since the lunar cycle is 29.5 days long, the Jewish calendar months alternate between 29 and 30 days in length. In a 29-day month, the process concludes a day earlier.

Source: *Likutei Sichot* 34, pp. 48–50

## *Months*

This chart presents the months of the Jewish calendar together with their respective themes, as explained by the Rebbe.

| MONTH | THEME |
|---|---|
| NISAN | Nisan is the month of redemption—both from the Egyptian exile and, in the future, from all exiles. The name "Nisan" contains two *nun* letters, alluding to *nisei nisim*, double miracles—Divine blessings that transcend the natural order. |
| IYAR | Iyar is an acronym for *Ani Hashem Rofecha*—"I am G-d your healer." In this month the trees are in full bloom, and the powers of nature are at their peak. The spiritual healing power of this month helps us overcome the challenges that nature poses to our Divine service and also manifests in physical healing. |
| SIVAN | The month of the giving of the Torah, Sivan is a time of unity—between Heaven and earth, and among the Jewish people. |
| TAMUZ | Tamuz is the hottest month of the year (in the Northern Hemisphere), when the sun shines at its brightest. Spiritually, this is when G-d's protection of the Jewish people is most openly revealed, "for the L-rd G-d is a sun and a shield" (Psalms 84:12). |
| MENACHEM AV | Av is a month of suffering, dominated by the Ninth of Av, the date of the destruction of the Temple. We refer to the month as Menachem Av, "the comforter of Av," because this month also has the power to transform our suffering into joy and bring us comfort. |
| ELUL | The month of Elul is a time of Divine accessibility. G-d meets us where we are—"in the field"—and shows us favor. At the same time, it is a mundane month without festivals, symbolizing that we cannot rely on inspiration from above; we must take the initiative to approach G-d ourselves. |

| MONTH | THEME |
|---|---|
| TISHREI | Beginning with the High Holidays, Tishrei is a month of repentance and prayer. The Divine revelation expressed by the holidays that fill this month inspires us and draws us closer to G-d. |
| CHESHVAN | Bereft of any festivals, Cheshvan represents Divine service within the routine of mundane life. Though more challenging, this type of service is the most meaningful and rewarding of all. |
| KISLEV | Kislev, the month of Chanukah—the Festival of Light—centers around the theme of the Torah's light. This is underscored by the 19th of Kislev, on which we celebrate the revelation of the deepest secrets of Torah, the teachings of *Chasidut*. |
| TEVET | The theme of Tevet is the mutual pleasure that G-d and the Jewish people derive from each other. G-d derives His deepest pleasure from our physical work and effort to serve Him. |
| SHEVAT | On the first day of the month of Shevat, Moses began expounding the Torah to the Jewish people one final time before his passing. He even explained the Torah in all of the seventy languages of the world. This gives Shevat its theme—spreading the teachings of Torah throughout the entire world. |
| ADAR | The month of Moses's birth, Adar is the luckiest month for the Jewish people. The festival of Purim makes the entire month a period of joy. |

**Sources**

Nisan: *Torat Menachem* 5744:3, p. 1422; Iyar: *Likutei Sichot* 32, pp. 72–76; Sivan: *Torat Menachem* 5717:3, p. 15, and 5742:3, p. 1491; Tamuz: *Torat Menachem* 5713:3, pp. 15–18; Menachem Av: 5712:3, p. 125; Elul: *Sefer Hamaamarim Melukat* 4, pp. 216–222; Tishrei: *Torat Menachem* 5715:2, pp. 276–289; Cheshvan: *Torat Menachem* 5743:1, pp. 490–495; Kislev: *Torat Menachem* 5717:1, pp. 75–78; Tevet: *Likutei Sichot* 15, pp. 382–383; Shevat: *Torat Menachem* 5746:2, p. 332; Adar: *Sefer Hasichot* 5752:2, p. 394

## The Fifty-Four *Parshiyot* of the Torah

The Torah is divided into fifty-four sections, known as *parshiyot*, which are read weekly in a year-long cycle.

| *PARSHAH* NAME | VERSES | TOPICS AND THEMES |
|---|---|---|
| | | **GENESIS** |
| **BERESHIT**<br>IN THE BEGINNING | 1:1–6:8 | G-d creates the world; Adam and Eve in the Garden of Eden; Cain murders Abel; the ten generations from Adam to Noah. |
| **NOACH**<br>NOAH | 6:9–11:32 | The Great Flood; the Tower of Babel; the seventy nations; the ten generations from Noah to Abraham. |
| **LECH LECHA**<br>GO YOU | 12:1–17:27 | Abraham and Sarah journey to the Holy Land; G-d's covenant with Abraham and his descendants; Hagar and Ishmael; Abraham's circumcision. |
| **VAYERA**<br>AND HE REVEALED HIMSELF | 18:1–22:24 | Visit of the three angels; destruction of Sodom; birth of Isaac; the binding of Isaac; the birth of Rebecca. |
| **CHAYEI SARAH**<br>THE LIFE OF SARAH | 23:1–25:18 | The passing and burial of Sarah; the marriage of Isaac and Rebecca. |
| **TOLEDOT**<br>PROGENY | 25:19–28:9 | Jacob and Esau; Isaac in the land of the Philistines; Jacob steals the blessings. |
| **VAYETZEI**<br>AND HE WENT OUT | 28:10–32:3 | Jacob's dream; Jacob's twenty years in Charan; his marriages to Leah and Rachel; the birth of eleven of the twelve tribes of Israel. |
| **VAYISHLACH**<br>AND HE SENT | 32:4–36:43 | Jacob's encounter with Esau; the rape of Dinah and the massacre of Shechem; Jacob is given the name "Israel"; the progeny of Esau. |

| | | |
|---|---|---|
| **VAYESHEV**<br>AND HE SETTLED | 37:1-40:23 | Joseph is sold into slavery by his brothers; the incident of Judah and Tamar; Joseph is libeled and imprisoned after rejecting the advances of Potiphar's wife. |
| **MIKETZ**<br>AT THE END | 41:1-44:17 | Pharaoh's dreams; Joseph is appointed viceroy of Egypt; Joseph's brothers come to Egypt to purchase grain during the seven years of famine; Joseph tests his brothers by threatening to keep Benjamin as a slave. |
| **VAYIGASH**<br>AND HE APPROACHED | 44:18-47:27 | Joseph reveals his identity to his brothers; Jacob and his family come down to Egypt. |
| **VAYECHI**<br>AND HE LIVED | 47:28-50:26 | Passing of Jacob and his blessings to his children; the passing of Joseph; the promise of redemption. |

## EXODUS

| | | |
|---|---|---|
| **SHEMOT**<br>NAMES | 1:1-6:1 | Enslavement in Egypt; birth and early years of Moses; Moses at the burning bush; Moses and Aaron confront Pharaoh. |
| **VA'ERA**<br>AND I REVEALED MYSELF | 6:2-9:35 | The first seven plagues brought upon Egypt. |
| **BO**<br>COME IN | 10:1-13:16 | The last three plagues; the Exodus from Egypt; the observances of Passover; consecration of the firstborn; the *mitzvah* of *tefilin*. |
| **BESHALACH**<br>WHEN HE SENT OUT | 13:17-17:16 | Splitting of the sea; the manna; the war with Amalek. |
| **YITRO**<br>JETHRO | 18:1-20:23 | Jethro visits the Israelite camp; the giving of the Torah at Mount Sinai; the Ten Commandments. |
| **MISHPATIM**<br>JUDGMENTS | 21:1-24:18 | Civil laws and torts given at Mount Sinai. |

| | | |
|---|---|---|
| **TERUMAH**<br>UPLIFTING | 25:1-27:19 | G-d instructs Moses on the building of the Tabernacle. |
| **TETZAVEH**<br>YOU SHALL COMMAND | 27:20-30:10 | The instructions to Moses on the making of the priestly garments and on the inauguration of the Tabernacle. |
| **KI TISA**<br>WHEN YOU RAISE UP | 30:11-34:35 | Worship of the Golden Calf; Moses breaks the Tablets of the Covenant; the Second Tablets. |
| **VAYAK'HEL**<br>AND HE ASSEMBLED | 35:1-38:20 | Making of the Tabernacle. |
| **PEKUDEI**<br>ACCOUNTINGS* | 38:21-40:38 | Making of the priestly garments; Tabernacle assembled. |

## LEVITICUS

| | | |
|---|---|---|
| **VAYIKRA**<br>AND HE CALLED | 1:1-5:26 | Laws of the *korbanot* (animal and meal offerings brought in the Tabernacle and in the Holy Temple). |
| **TZAV**<br>COMMAND | 6:1-8:36 | More laws of *korbanot*; preparations for the Tabernacle's inauguration. |
| **SHEMINI**<br>EIGHTH | 9:1-11:47 | Inauguration of the Tabernacle; death of Nadab and Abihu; the kosher dietary laws. |
| **TAZRIA**<br>SHE SHALL SEED | 12:1-13:59 | Laws pertaining to childbirth; laws of *tzaraat* ("leprosy"). |
| **METZORA**<br>LEPER* | 14:1-15:33 | Purification process of the leper; laws of *nidah* (menstruant). |
| **ACHAREI MOT**<br>AFTER THE DEATH | 16:1-18:30 | Yom Kippur service in the Holy Temple; prohibitions against incest and other forbidden relations. |

| | | |
|---|---|---|
| **KEDOSHIM**<br>HOLY ONES* | 19:1-20:27 | Numerous *mitzvot,* including laws pertaining to honesty in business, agricultural gifts to the poor, the prohibition of gossip and slander; and the rule "Love your fellow as yourself" introduced. |
| **EMOR**<br>SAY | 21:1-24:23 | Laws pertaining to the *Kohanim* (priests); the festivals of the Jewish year. |
| **BEHAR**<br>ON THE MOUNTAIN | 25:1-26:2 | Laws pertaining to the observance of the sabbatical and jubilee years, the sale of land, and prohibitions against fraud and usury. |
| **BECHUKOTAI**<br>IN MY STATUTES* | 26:3-27:34 | The rewards for keeping the Torah's commandments; the catastrophes destined to befall the people should they abandon their covenant with G-d; laws of pledges to the Temple and animal tithes. |

## NUMBERS

| | | |
|---|---|---|
| **BAMIDBAR**<br>IN THE WILDERNESS | 1:1-4:20 | The census taken of the people of Israel in the Sinai Desert. |
| **NASO**<br>LIFT UP | 4:21-7:89 | Populations of the Levite families; laws of the Nazirite and of the *sotah* (wayward wife); the priestly blessing; gifts brought by the tribal leaders for the dedication of the Tabernacle. |
| **BEHAALOTECHA**<br>WHEN YOU ELEVATE | 8:1-12:16 | Kindling of the Menorah; inauguration of the Levites' service in the Tabernacle; the Second Passover; description of the Israelites' encampment and journeys in the wilderness; the people criticize the manna and demand meat; Miriam punished for speaking negatively of Moses. |
| **SHELACH**<br>SEND | 13:1-15:41 | Spies sent to explore the Promised Land dissuade the people from entering the Land, and it is decreed that the generation of the Exodus will die out in the wilderness; the libations brought with the Temple offerings; the *mitzvah* of *tzitzit.* |

| | | |
|---|---|---|
| **KORACH**<br>KORAH | 16:1–18:32 | Korah's rebellion against Moses; the gifts and tithes given to the *Kohen* and Levite. |
| **CHUKAT**<br>THE STATUTE OF | 19:1–22:1 | Law of the Red Heifer; the passing of Miriam; Moses strikes the rock; the passing of Aaron; conquest of the Emorite lands east of the Jordan River. |
| **BALAK**<br>BALAK (MOABITE KING)* | 22:2–25:9 | Balaam's curses are transformed into blessings; the Israelites sin with the daughters of Moab and worship the idol Pe'or; Phinehas stops the plague by killing Zimri and the Midianite woman. |
| **PINCHAS**<br>PHINEHAS | 25:10–30:1 | Phinehas is rewarded for his act of zealotry; allotment of the Land of Israel among the tribes and families; the second census; the petition of the daughters of Zelophehad and the laws of inheritance; the daily and seasonal offerings brought in the Temple. |
| **MATOT**<br>TRIBES | 30:2–32:42 | Laws of the annulment of vows; the war on Midian; the tribes of Reuben and Gad ask to be granted the eastern territories. |
| **MASEI**<br>JOURNEYS* | 33:1–36:13 | List of the forty-two encampments of the Israelites in the forty-year journey from Egypt to the Promised Land; the boundaries of the Land; the "Cities of Refuge" set aside for one who kills by accident. |
| | **DEUTERONOMY** | |
| **DEVARIM**<br>WORDS | 1:1–3:22 | Moses begins his "repetition of the Torah" five weeks before his passing; he recounts the incident of the spies and the conquests of the lands of Sichon and Og. |
| **VA'ETCHANAN**<br>AND I IMPLORED | 3:23–7:11 | Moses implores G-d to allow him to enter the Land; the unity and exclusivity of G-d; description of the revelation at Mount Sinai and repetition of the Ten Commandments; the Shema. |

| | | |
|---|---|---|
| **EKEV**<br>IN CONSEQUENCE OF | 7:12–11:25 | The blessings of the Land of Israel; Moses recounts the people's forty-year journey through the wilderness; the second portion of the Shema. |
| **RE'EH**<br>SEE | 11:26–16:17 | The blessings and curses to be given on Mount Gerizim and Mount Ebal; worship in a Holy Temple in "the place that G-d will choose to make dwell His name"; the eradication of idolatry; the laws of prophecy; receipt of the kosher dietary laws; the *mitzvah* of charity; the three pilgrimage festivals. |
| **SHOFTIM**<br>JUDGES | 16:18–21:9 | Establishment of a justice system; the principle of equality before the law; laws governing the conduct of a king; laws of warfare. |
| **KI TETZEI**<br>WHEN YOU GO OUT | 21:10–25:19 | Contains seventy-four *mitzvot* including the laws of marriage and divorce, employee rights, return of a lost object, burial and dignity of the dead, and forbidden plant and animal hybrids (*kilayim*). |
| **KI TAVO**<br>WHEN YOU COME IN | 26:1–29:8 | The gift of "first fruits" brought to the Temple; warning of the calamities to befall the people of Israel if they fail to keep the Torah. |
| **NITZAVIM**<br>STANDING ERECT | 29:9–30:20 | The unity of Israel; the Future Redemption; the principle of free choice. |
| **VAYELECH**<br>AND HE WENT* | 31:1–30 | On the last day of his life, Moses transfers the leadership to Joshua; transcribes the Torah and presents it to the people. |
| **HAAZINU**<br>LISTEN | 32:1–52 | The song delivered by Moses recounting the history of the people of Israel and their future travails. |
| **VEZOT HABERACHAH**<br>AND THIS IS THE BLESSING | 33:1–34:12 | Moses's blessings to the twelve tribes of Israel; the passing of Moses. |

*Depending on calendrical considerations, in certain years this portion is read together with the previous one, on the same Shabbat.

**EXERCISE 4.3**

Using the information provided in "The Jewish Map of Time," create a time profile for the date on which this class is taking place. Identify the various spiritual energies associated with today—based on the Hebrew month, week, and date—and use those insights to develop your own personal "order of the day."

## IV. PERSONAL TIME

Time also holds special significance on the personal level. Certain days are uniquely meaningful for the individual—particularly their birthday.

**TEXT 7**

### Re-birthdays

The Rebbe, Rabbi Menachem Mendel Schneerson,
*Sefer Hasichot* 5748:2, pp. 401–402

עִנְיַן הַשִּׂמְחָה וּנְתִינַת שֶׁבַח וְהוֹדָיָה כוּ' בְּיוֹם הַהוּלֶּדֶת דְּכָל אֶחָד וְאַחַת מִיִּשְׂרָאֵל, הוּא – לֹא רַק בְּיַחַס לַמְאוֹרָע דְּהַלֵּידָה בַּפַּעַם הָרִאשׁוֹנָה (שֶׁנִּזְכַּר בְּיוֹם זֶה), אֶלָּא גַם בְּיַחַס לְעִנְיַן הַלֵּידָה **שֶׁנַּעֲשֶׂה** בְּיוֹם זֶה מַמָּשׁ, שֶׁחוֹזֵר וְנִשְׁנָה הַמְשָׁכַת חַיּוּתוֹ . . . הַמְשָׁכַת חַיּוּת חָדָשׁ עַל כָּל הַשָּׁנָה כּוּלָּהּ.

The joy—and the offering of praise and thanks to G-d on the birthday of every individual Jew—is not only in connection to the original event of their birth (which is commemorated on this day) but also in connection to the birth that takes place on this very day itself—when their vitality is once again drawn down . . . a new flow of life-force for the entire year ahead.

**RABBI MENACHEM MENDEL SCHNEERSON 1902–1994**

The towering Jewish leader of the 20th century, known as "the Lubavitcher Rebbe," or simply as "the Rebbe." Born in southern Ukraine, the Rebbe escaped Nazi-occupied Europe, arriving in the U.S. in June 1941. The Rebbe inspired and guided the revival of traditional Judaism after the European devastation, impacting virtually every Jewish community the world over. The Rebbe often emphasized that the performance of just one additional good deed could usher in the era of Mashiach. The Rebbe's scholarly talks and writings have been printed in more than 200 volumes.

FIGURE 4.1

## Birthday Practices

A ten-point program suggested by the Lubavitcher Rebbe, Rabbi Menachem Mendel Schneerson

---

**Men: Arrange to be called up to the Torah in the synagogue on the Shabbat before your Jewish birthday.**

---

**Give extra charity on this day. (If your birthday is on Shabbat or a festival day, do so on the preceding day.)**

---

**Pray with increased concentration, and read from the book of Psalms.**

---

**Read and study the chapter in Psalms that corresponds with the years of your life (e.g., on your thirtieth birthday, study Psalm 31, as you are entering your thirty-first year).**

---

**Study Torah texts (in addition to your regular study schedule).**

---

**Learn a text from the mystical portion of the Torah, and repeat it to others.**

---

**Find a way to lovingly and respectfully have a positive influence on another person.**

---

**Set aside a time for private contemplation and stocktaking of the previous year, resolving to correct any wrongdoings and to find ways to improve yourself.**

---

**Undertake a new *mitzvah* or positive practice in honor of your birthday.**

---

**Get together with family and friends to joyously celebrate and express your gratitude to G-d.**

## KEY POINTS

1. Judaism teaches that each day carries its own spiritual energy, and by aligning with the rhythms of time, even routine actions are infused with new vitality.

2. The sacredness of Jewish holidays and special occasions is not merely a projection; the time itself is inherently holy. This is an objective reality. The holiness of these days is not something we *create*, but something we *enter*.

3. Jewish holidays are opportunities to access spiritual wells revealed through history. Each holiday brings its own Divine energy, which we tap into through the *mitzvot*, prayers, and rituals that define the day.

4. Beyond holidays and special occasions, every day of the week and date on the calendar also carries its own spiritual significance.

5. A birthday is an annual return of the spiritual force that brought you into existence. The Rebbe encouraged Jews to embrace their birthdays and outlined a set of meaningful practices for that day.

## Psychology References

Bryant, F. B., & Veroff, J. (2007). *Savoring: A new model of positive experience.* Lawrence Erlbaum Associates, Mahwah, N.J.

Klibert, J. J., et al. (2022). Savoring interventions increase positive emotions after a social-evaluative hassle. *Frontiers in Psychology*, 13, Article 791040.

Dai, H., & Li, C. (2019). How experiencing and anticipating temporal landmarks influence motivation. *Current Opinion in Psychology*, 26, 44–48.

Pluut, H., et al. (2022). Development and validation of a short measure of emotional, physical, and behavioral markers of eustress and distress (MEDS). *Healthcare*, 10(2), 339.

Kloidt, J., & Barsalou, L. W. (2024). Establishing a comprehensive hierarchical construct of eustress (CHE). *Current Psychology*, 43, 32258–32273.

Brick, D. J., et al. (2023). Celebrate good times: How celebrations increase perceived social support. *Journal of Consumer Psychology,* 34(1), 33–55.

Bytheway, B. (2009). Writing about age, birthdays, and the passage of time. *Ageing and Society*. 2009; 29(6):883–901.

LESSON 5

## MEANING IN THE UNCHOSEN

*Some things are clearly meaningful, but what if everything is? Explore a vision of life where every event and circumstance catalyzes growth and leads to greater purpose.*

**SEARCHING FOR THE SPARKS (DETAIL)**
Berit Engen, woven tapestry, linen yarn, Oak Park, Illinois, 2009

## I. INTRODUCTION

Our previous lessons focused on how we can create meaning in our lives. But not every part of life is chosen, and things don't always go according to plan. In the present lesson, we'll explore what it means to live meaningfully not just through what we do but through how we receive, respond, and grow when life surprises us.

**WEATHERING THE STORM**
Rochelle Blumenfeld (1936–2025), acrylic on canvas, Pittsburgh, Pennsylvania

EXERCISE 5.1

## Meaning Audit: Action vs. Experience

**List 2–3 recent things you *chose* to do that felt meaningful.**

*Examples: I visited someone in the hospital.*
*I spent time learning Torah.*

1.
2.
3.

**List 2–3 recent things that *happened* to you.**

*Examples: I got stuck in traffic.*
*There was a major news event I couldn't stop thinking about.*

1.
2.
3.

**Take a few moments to reflect:**

- **Which list feels more personal?**
- **Which moments felt more meaningful—immediately or in retrospect?**
- **What made them meaningful, or not?**

## II. WHEN YOU'RE NOT THE ONE WRITING THE SCRIPT

The key to finding meaning in the circumstances we experience lies in understanding the extent and degree of G-d's role in shaping them.

**TEXT 1**

### G-d's Script

Maimonides, Mishnah, Sanhedrin, ch. 10, Introduction, Thirteen Principles of Faith, First Principle

אֲנִי מַאֲמִין בֶּאֱמוּנָה שְׁלֵמָה שֶׁהַבּוֹרֵא יִתְבָּרַךְ שְׁמוֹ הוּא בּוֹרֵא וּמַנְהִיג לְכָל הַבְּרוּאִים. וְהוּא לְבַדּוֹ עָשָׂה וְעוֹשֶׂה וְיַעֲשֶׂה לְכָל הַמַּעֲשִׂים.

I believe with complete faith that the Creator, blessed be His name, is the Creator and Guide of all created beings. He alone made, makes, and will make all things.

**RABBI MOSHE BEN MAIMON (MAIMONIDES, RAMBAM) 1135–1204**

Halachist, philosopher, author, and physician. Maimonides was born in Córdoba, Spain. After the conquest of Córdoba by the Almohads, he fled Spain and eventually settled in Cairo, Egypt. There, he became the leader of the Jewish community and served as court physician to the vizier of Egypt. He is most noted for authoring the *Mishneh Torah*, an encyclopedic arrangement of Jewish law; and for his philosophical work, *Guide for the Perplexed*. His rulings on Jewish law are integral to the formation of Halachic consensus.

**TEXT 2**

## Spiritual Wiring

Lisa Miller, PhD, *The Awakened Brain: The New Science of Spirituality and Our Quest for an Inspired Life* (New York, N.Y.: Random House, 2021), pp. 7–9

Each of us is endowed with a natural capacity to perceive a greater reality and consciously connect to the life force that moves in, through, and around us. Whether or not we participate in a spiritual practice or adhere to a faith tradition, whether or not we identify as religious or spiritual, our brain has a natural inclination toward and a docking station for spiritual awareness. . . .

An awakened brain is available to all of us, right here in our neural circuitry. But we have to choose to engage it. It's a muscle we can learn to strengthen, or let atrophy.

**LISA MILLER, PHD**

Psychologist and author. Lisa Miller serves as a professor of psychology and education at Teachers College, Columbia University, and is the founder of the Spirituality Mind Body Institute, a graduate program in spirituality and psychology. Her research focuses on the quantifiable effects of spirituality in mental health, and she is the author of *The Spiritual Child* and *The Awakened Brain*.

**TEXT 3**

## Continually Renewing

*Siddur Tehillat Hashem*, Morning Prayer

הַמְחַדֵּשׁ בְּטוּבוֹ בְּכָל יוֹם תָּמִיד מַעֲשֵׂה בְרֵאשִׁית. כָּאָמוּר:
"לְעוֹשֵׂה אוֹרִים גְּדוֹלִים כִּי לְעוֹלָם חַסְדּוֹ" (תְּהִלִּים קלו, ז).

In His goodness, G-d renews each day, continually, the act of Creation, as it is said: "[Give thanks] to He Who makes great luminaries, for His kindness is eternal" (PSALMS 136:7).

***SIDDUR TEHILLAT HASHEM***

One of the prayer books that follow the tradition of the Arizal, as established by Rabbi Shneur Zalman of Liadi. It was first published in New York in 1945.

TEXT 4

## Continually Renewing

Rabbi Yeshayahu Halevi Horowitz, *Shenei Luchot Haberit, Asarah Maamarot, Maamar* 1

הִנֵּה סְבָרַת הָעוֹלָם הִיא בְּעִנְיַן מַעֲרֶכֶת צְבָא הַשָּׁמַיִם כָּךְ: הַבּוֹרֵא בָּרוּךְ הוּא חִידֵּשׁ הַכֹּל יֵשׁ מֵאַיִן הַמּוּחְלָט, עַל כֵּן בִּיכָלְתּוֹ לַעֲשׂוֹת מָה שֶׁרוֹצֶה לְשַׁנּוֹת וּלְשַׁדֵּד. בְּרֵאשִׁית נָתַן הַקָּדוֹשׁ בָּרוּךְ הוּא לִצְבָא הַשָּׁמַיִם כֹּחַ וִיכוֹלֶת לְהַנְהִיג הָעוֹלָם, וְכָל כּוֹכָב מְמוּנֶּה עַל מִינוֹ שֶׁלוֹ, הָעוֹלָם כְּמִנְהָגוֹ נוֹהֵג וְכִבְיָכוֹל זָזָה יָדוֹ מֵהֶם, רַק אִם לְעֵת מֵהָעִתִּים רוֹצֶה לְשַׁדֵּד אוֹתָם. וְכָל זְמַן שֶׁאֵינוֹ מְשַׁדֵּד, אָז מַנְהִיגָם בְּכֹחַ שֶׁהוּשַּׂג לָהֶם בְּעֵת הַבְּרִיאָה.

אָמְנָם אֲמִיתַּת הָאֱמוּנָה הַנִּרְאֶה בְּעֵינַי הִיא, הַשֵּׁם יִתְבָּרַךְ מְחַדֵּשׁ בְּטוּבוֹ בְּכָל יוֹם תָּמִיד מַעֲשֵׂה בְרֵאשִׁית בְּכַוָּנָה מְכֻוֶּנֶת שׁוֹפֵעַ שִׁפְעוֹ, וְאִלּוּ הָיָה מוֹנֵעַ רֶגַע אֶחָד הָיָה הַכֹּל כְּלֹא הָיָה, בָּטֵל הַמְּצִיאוּת.

The common understanding of how the Heavenly forces operate is this: G-d, the blessed Creator, brought everything into being from absolute nothingness and, therefore, has the power to do whatever He wills, even to override or suspend the natural order. At the outset, He assigned spiritual forces to govern the world, each one appointed over its own realm. The world continues to function according to these systems, as if His hand has stepped back—except on such occasions when He chooses to intervene and override them. Until

**RABBI YESHAYAHU HALEVI HOROWITZ (*SHALAH*) 1565–1630**

Kabbalist and author. Rabbi Horowitz was born in Prague and served as rabbi in several prominent Jewish communities, including Frankfurt am Main and his native Prague. After the passing of his wife in 1620, he moved to Israel. In Tiberias, he completed his *Shenei Luchot Haberit*, an encyclopedic compilation of kabbalistic ideas. He is buried in Tiberias, next to Maimonides.

then, these forces operate through the power He originally placed within them at the time of Creation.

But in truth, as it seems to me, our faith teaches otherwise. G-d, in His goodness, is constantly and deliberately renewing the act of Creation every single day. His influence is ongoing and intentional. If, for even a moment, He were to withdraw this flow, everything would immediately dissolve into nothingness. All of existence would simply cease.

**TEXT 5**

## Holding It Together

Rabbi Shneur Zalman of Liadi, *Tanya, Shaar Hayichud Veha'emunah*, ch. 2

וְהִנֵּה מִכָּאן תְּשׁוּבַת הַמִּינִים וְגִילּוּי שׁוֹרֶשׁ טָעוּתָם הַכּוֹפְרִים בְּהַשְׁגָּחָה פְּרָטִית וּבְאוֹתוֹת וּמוֹפְתֵי הַתּוֹרָה. שֶׁטּוֹעִים בְּדִמְיוֹנָם הַכּוֹזֵב, שֶׁמְּדַמִּין מַעֲשֵׂה ה', עוֹשֶׂה שָׁמַיִם וָאָרֶץ, לְמַעֲשֵׂה אֱנוֹשׁ וְתַחְבּוּלוֹתָיו. כִּי כַּאֲשֶׁר יָצָא לַצּוֹרֵף כְּלִי, שׁוּב אֵין הַכְּלִי צָרִיךְ לִידֵי הַצּוֹרֵף, כִּי אַף שֶׁיָּדָיו מְסוּלָּקוֹת הֵימֶנּוּ וְהוֹלֵךְ לוֹ בַּשּׁוּק, הַכְּלִי קַיָּים בְּתַבְנִיתוֹ וְצַלְמוֹ מַמָּשׁ כַּאֲשֶׁר יָצָא מִיְּדֵי הַצּוֹרֵף. כָּךְ מְדַמִּין הַסְּכָלִים הָאֵלּוּ מַעֲשֵׂה שָׁמַיִם וָאָרֶץ.

אַךְ טָח מֵרְאוֹת עֵינֵיהֶם הַהֶבְדֵּל הַגָּדוֹל שֶׁבֵּין מַעֲשֵׂה אֱנוֹשׁ וְתַחְבּוּלוֹתָיו, שֶׁהוּא יֵשׁ מִיֵּשׁ רַק שֶׁמְּשַׁנֶּה הַצּוּרָה וְהַתְּמוּנָה מִתְּמוּנַת חֲתִיכַת כֶּסֶף לִתְמוּנַת כְּלִי, לְמַעֲשֵׂה שָׁמַיִם וָאָרֶץ שֶׁהוּא יֵשׁ מֵאַיִן. וְהוּא פֶּלֶא גָּדוֹל יוֹתֵר

**RABBI SHNEUR ZALMAN OF LIADI (ALTER REBBE) 1745–1812**

Chasidic rebbe, Halachic authority, and founder of the Chabad movement. The Alter Rebbe was born in Liozna, Belarus, and was among the principal students of the Magid of Mezeritch. His numerous works include the *Tanya*, an early classic containing the fundamentals of Chabad Chasidism; and *Shulchan Aruch HaRav*, an expanded and reworked code of Jewish law.

מִקְרִיעַת יַם סוּף עַל דֶּרֶךְ מָשָׁל, שֶׁהוֹלִיךְ ה׳ אֶת הַיָּם בְּרוּחַ
קָדִים עַזָּה כָּל הַלַּיְלָה וַיִּבָּקְעוּ הַמַּיִם וְנִצְבוּ כְּמוֹ נֵד וּכְחוֹמָה,
וְאִילוּ הִפְסִיק ה׳ אֶת הָרוּחַ כְּרֶגַע, הָיוּ הַמַּיִם חוֹזְרִים וְנִיגָּרִים
בַּמּוֹרָד כְּדַרְכָּם וְטִבְעָם וְלֹא קָמוּ כְּחוֹמָה בְּלִי סָפֵק . . .

וְכָל שֶׁכֵּן וְקַל וָחוֹמֶר בִּבְרִיאַת יֵשׁ מֵאַיִן, שֶׁהִיא לְמַעְלָה
מֵהַטֶּבַע וְהַפְלֵא וָפֶלֶא יוֹתֵר מִקְרִיעַת יַם סוּף, עַל אַחַת
כַּמָּה וְכַמָּה שֶׁבְּהִסְתַּלְּקוּת כֹּחַ הַבּוֹרֵא מִן הַנִּבְרָא חַס
וְשָׁלוֹם יָשׁוּב הַנִּבְרָא לְאַיִן וְאֶפֶס מַמָּשׁ, אֶלָּא צָרִיךְ
לִהְיוֹת כֹּחַ הַפּוֹעֵל בַּנִּפְעָל תָּמִיד לְהַחֲיוֹתוֹ וּלְקַיְּימוֹ.

This idea offers a clear response to those who deny Divine providence and the miracles of the Torah. Their mistake lies in a false comparison: They imagine that G-d's Creation of the heavens and the earth is like human craftsmanship. Just as a craftsperson might make a vessel and then walk away, with the vessel remaining intact without the artisan's ongoing involvement, they assume the same is true of the world—that once created, it runs on its own.

But they fail to see a critical difference. When humans create something, they're not creating from nothing: they just reshape existing material, like turning a piece of silver into a utensil. But G-d created the world out of absolute nothingness. That's a far greater wonder—even more astounding than the Splitting of the Sea.

Take that miracle as an example: G-d used a strong east wind to split the sea, and the waters stood like a wall. But if the wind had stopped for even a moment, the waters would have immediately returned to their natural state and flowed back down, and they would not have continued standing as a wall on their own.

So how much more so with creation itself, which is something from nothing. That's beyond nature and an even greater miracle than the Splitting of the Sea. If G-d were to stop sustaining the world for even a moment, G-d forbid, it would vanish into nothingness. The world continues to exist only because His creative energy is constantly present within it, giving it life every second.

**TEXT 6**

## Providence and the Rolling Leaf

Rabbi Yosef Yitzchak Schneersohn,
*Likutei Diburim* 1, p. 83b

דֶער בַּעַל שֵׁם טוֹב אִיז מְבָאֵר, אַז אֲפִילוּ אַ שְׁטְרוֹיֶעלֶע אוּן אַ אָפְּגֶעְרִיסֶענֶע בְּלֶעטֶעלֶע וָואס וָואלְגֶערְט זִיךְ אִין גַאס, אִיז פַּארַאן אַ דִין וּמִשְׁפָּט וְוִיפִיל מָאל זֵיי זָאלְן זִיךְ אוּמדְרֶעהֶען אוּן ווּאוּ, אִין וָואסֶערֶע עֶרטֶער זֵיי זָאלֶען זִיךְ וָואלְגֶערֶען.

The Baal Shem Tov explains that even a piece of straw or a torn leaf rolling in the street is subject to Divine judgment: there is a decree for exactly how many times it should turn over, where it should roll, and in which places it should end up.

**RABBI YOSEF YITZCHAK SCHNEERSOHN (RAYATZ, FRIERDIKER REBBE, PREVIOUS REBBE) 1880–1950**

Chasidic rebbe, prolific writer, and Jewish activist. Rabbi Yosef Yitzchak, the 6th leader of the Chabad movement, actively promoted Jewish religious practice in Soviet Russia and was arrested for these activities. After his release from prison and exile, he settled in Warsaw, Poland, from where he fled Nazi occupation and arrived in New York in 1940. Settling in Brooklyn, Rabbi Schneersohn worked to revitalize American Jewish life. His son-in-law Rabbi Menachem Mendel Schneerson succeeded him as the leader of the Chabad movement.

FIGURE 5.1

## *Hashgachah* vs. *Hashgachah Peratit* Mindsets

| SCENARIO | | |
|---|---|---|
| You're sitting in an airport, and the screen flashes: *Flight delayed—3 hours.* | | |
| ***HASHGACHAH* MINDSET** *(There must be a reason.)* | ***HASHGACHAH PERATIT* MINDSET I** *(There must be a reason that is meant for me.)* | ***HASHGACHAH PERATIT* MINDSET II** *(There must also be a reason for all the details of the situation.)* |
| Okay, take a deep breath: This is from G-d! Maybe there's someone who is running late who absolutely must make this flight for reasons of geopolitical importance. This delay will allow them to make this flight. I'll try to be patient—G-d runs the world and is also watching to make sure I'll be fine. | The delay must (also) be meaningful for me. Maybe it's protecting me from something. Maybe something was going to go wrong with the weather if it were to have departed on time. Maybe the meeting I was supposed to attend and that I will now miss would not have been beneficial for me. Or maybe He's just giving me time to finally finish that book I started reading in 2009. | In addition to all the previous truths about the reason for the delay, there's a reason I'm meant to be here, now, at this exact gate, at this exact hour. Maybe I'll end up talking to the woman sitting next to me, and she's someone I'm meant to meet. Maybe I'll learn something from watching the way someone handles their stress. Maybe the book I'm about to read during this delay will spark an idea that changes how I think. |

**SCENARIO**

You're looking for a new house in an area you'd love to move to, but you can't find a house to fit your needs (or the only house you find in your price range fails inspection, or someone else outbids you . . . or . . .).

| ***HASHGACHAH* MINDSET** | ***HASHGACHAH PERATIT* MINDSET I** | ***HASHGACHAH PERATIT* MINDSET II** |
|---|---|---|
| Maybe someone else needed that house more urgently—perhaps a family in crisis or someone whose livelihood depended on being in that location. Maybe this entire area is part of a larger shift that G-d is orchestrating for reasons beyond me. I don't know the full picture, but I trust that He does. | Not only is there a reason this house didn't work out—there's a reason *I* am being blocked. Maybe there's another home that's better suited to my needs. Maybe this delay is timed to something I can't yet see. | There's a reason I toured that exact house, met that specific realtor, and saw what I saw. Maybe a comment I heard will shape a future decision. Maybe I'm meant to reconnect with someone I bumped into during the search. Even the timing of the inspection or the particular emotion I felt walking away: none of it is accidental. |

**SCENARIO**

You're rushing out the door to the office, juggling your keys and your phone, and right outside your building you spill your coffee all over yourself. You're frustrated. You're late. Your clothes are stained.

| ***HASHGACHAH* MINDSET** | ***HASHGACHAH PERATIT* MINDSET I** | ***HASHGACHAH PERATIT* MINDSET II** |
|---|---|---|
| Well, this must be for a reason. I was supposed to close a deal at the office, but maybe the company I work for was not meant to make that deal: maybe the company was not supposed to make that profit, or maybe a better deal for the company is waiting elsewhere. | There has to be a reason why I am late (independent of the effect it may have on my company). Maybe if I had left on time, I would've walked into a dangerous situation. Maybe this is G-d sending me an important message, telling me that I need to slow down. | In addition to all the above, there is a reason I needed to spill this coffee, on my clothing, causing me to need to be an extra few minutes in my home. What could that be? |

**EXERCISE 5.2**

**Add another hypothetical scenario to the *Hashgachah* vs. *Hashgachah Peratit* Mindset.**

| SCENARIO | |
|---|---|
| | |
| ***HASHGACHAH* MINDSET** *(There must be a reason.)* | |
| ***HASHGACHAH PERATIT* MINDSET I** *(There must be a reason that is meant for me.)* | |
| ***HASHGACHAH PERATIT* MINDSET II** *(There must also be a reason for all the details of the situation.)* | |

## III. HOW TO FIND THE PURPOSE

Having established that everything that happens to us has meaning and purpose, we now turn to explore how we can identify that purpose.

**MELODY**
Nathan Brutsky (b. 1963, Kiev, Ukraine), Tel Aviv

TEXT 7

## Lifelong Impact

Beth Kurland, PhD, "How You Can Make an Impact in 30 Seconds Without Knowing It," www.psychologytoday.com

On the day of my mother's funeral, I remember sitting in the back seat of our car, pulling into the parking lot where the service was going to be held, and seeing two old friends of mine from elementary school walking inside. I was 15 at the time. It had never occurred to me that they would miss school to be there for me. This simple act of support meant more to me than they will ever know.

**BETH KURLAND, PHD**

Psychologist and author. Beth Kurland received her PhD in clinical psychology from Clark University and has been practicing as a psychologist in Norwood, Massachusetts for over three decades. She emphasizes the benefits of meditation and mind-body practices and is the author of three books, including *You Don't Have to Change to Change Everything: Six Ways to Shift Your Vantage Point.*

**TWO WOMEN**
Avraham Goldberg (1906–1980), oil on wood, Israel

**TEXT 8**

## Oblivious Effect

The Rebbe, Rabbi Menachem Mendel Schneerson, *Torat Menachem* 5715:2 (14), pp. 192–194

כְּבוֹד קְדֻשַּׁת מוֹרִי וְחָמִי אֲדוֹנֵנוּ מוֹרֵנוּ וְרַבֵּנוּ הִנְהִיג מִכַּמָּה שָׁנִים, שֶׁבִּימֵי הַקַּיִץ נוֹסְעִים מֵהַיְשִׁיבָה בַּחוּרִים שֶׁמִּתְנַדְּבִים לְבַקֵּר בְּמוֹשְׁבוֹת בְּנֵי יִשְׂרָאֵל לְעוֹרֵר אוֹתָם עַל עִנְיְנֵי תּוֹרָה וּמִצְווֹת וְיַהֲדוּת בִּכְלָל. וּמִסְתָּמָא נִתְקַבְּלָה כְּבָר אֶצְלָם הַהַחְלָטָה לִנְסוֹעַ בְּשָׁעָה טוֹבָה וּמוּצְלַחַת . . . שֶׁהַנְּסִיעָה תִּהְיֶה לֹא רַק לְשָׁלוֹם, אֶלָּא גַּם בְּהַצְלָחָה, וְלֹא רַק הַצְלָחָה סְתָם, אֶלָּא הַצְלָחָה מוּפְלָגָה בְּכָל הָעִנְיָנִים שֶׁאוֹדוֹתָם יְדַבְּרוּ, וַאֲפִילוּ בְּהָעִנְיָנִים שֶׁלֹּא יְדַבְּרוּ, אֶלָּא יֵיעָשׂוּ מִצַּד עֶצֶם שֶׁהוּתָם בִּמְקוֹמוֹת אֵלוּ.

וְכַיָּדוּעַ הַסִּיפּוּר מָה שֶׁנִּפְעַל אֵצֶל יְהוּדִי שֶׁגָּר בַּעֲיָרָה אֲמֵרִיקָאִית, כְּתוֹצָאָה מִזֶּה שֶׁעָבַר שָׁם בָּחוּר עָטוּר זָקָן וּפֵאוֹת וְצִיצִיּוֹתָיו גְּלוּיוֹת, וְכַאֲשֶׁר הַלָּה הִתְעַנְיֵין לְמוֹצָאוֹ שֶׁל הַבָּחוּר הַנִּזְכָּר לְעֵיל, הַאִם הוּא מִפּוֹלִין, גָּלִיצְיָה אוֹ אוּקְרָאִינָה, אָמְרוּ לוֹ, שֶׁהוּא אֶחָד מֵהַ"בָּאסְטָאנִיעֶנְס"!

- בִּמְדִינָה זוֹ נֶחֱשָׁבִים הַ"בָּאסְטָאנִיעֶנְס" כְּאֵלֶּה שֶׁאֵין לְמַעְלָה מֵהֶם . . . וּמַה גָּדְלָה הַפְתָּעָתוֹ לִשְׁמוֹעַ שֶׁגַּם הַבָּחוּר הַנִּזְכָּר לְעֵיל הוּא "בָּאסְטָאנִיעֶן", וְאַף עַל פִּי כֵן, הוֹלֵךְ הוּא עָטוּר פֵּיאוֹת וְזָקָן שָׁלֵם, וְצִיצִיּוֹתָיו גְּלוּיוֹת, וּמְדַבֵּר הוּא - בְּאַנְגְּלִית רְהוּטָה - אוֹדוֹת עִנְיָנִים שֶׁל יִחוּדָא עִילָּאָה וְיִחוּדָא תַּתָּאָה! . . .

**RABBI MENACHEM MENDEL SCHNEERSON 1902–1994**

The towering Jewish leader of the 20th century, known as "the Lubavitcher Rebbe," or simply as "the Rebbe." Born in southern Ukraine, the Rebbe escaped Nazi-occupied Europe, arriving in the U.S. in June 1941. The Rebbe inspired and guided the revival of traditional Judaism after the European devastation, impacting virtually every Jewish community the world over. The Rebbe often emphasized that the performance of just one additional good deed could usher in the era of Mashiach. The Rebbe's scholarly talks and writings have been printed in more than 200 volumes.

וְעִנְיָן זֶה פָּעַל עָלָיו: לְכָל לְרֹאשׁ הִרְוִיחַ הַ"מְשׁוּלָּח" שֶׁהִגִּיעַ לְאַחֲרֵי הַבָּחוּר - שֶׁהַלָּה הוֹסִיף לוֹ עוֹד כַּמָּה דוֹלָרִים; וְעוֹד זֹאת, שֶׁלְּאַחֲרֵי כֵּן הָיוּ יְכוֹלִים לִפְעוֹל עָלָיו בְּנוֹגֵעַ לְכַשְׁרוּת, וּלְאַחֲרֵי כֵּן - "לְאַט לְאַט אֲגָרְשֶׁנּוּ" - גַּם בְּנוֹגֵעַ לְעִנְיָנִים נוֹסָפִים שֶׁל מִצְווֹת מַעֲשִׂיּוֹת.

וְסָבִיר לְהָנִיחַ שֶׁהַבָּחוּר הַנִּזְכָּר לְעֵיל שֶׁגָּרַם לְכָל זֶה - אֵינוֹ יוֹדֵעַ מִזֶּה עַד הַיּוֹם!

My father-in-law, the [Previous] Rebbe [Rabbi Yosef Yitzchak Schneersohn], instituted several years ago that during the summer months, yeshiva students would volunteer to travel from the yeshiva to various Jewish communities in order to inspire their fellow Jews in matters of Torah, *mitzvot*, and Judaism in general. Presumably, the yeshiva students have already decided to embark on this mission in a good and auspicious hour. . . . May the trip be not only peaceful but also successful—not just successful in a general sense but remarkably successful in all areas in which they will speak, and even in areas in which they won't speak but will influence simply through their very presence in these places.

There is a story that illustrates this: A Jew living in a small American town was deeply affected just by the sight of a young man walking by—wearing a full beard and *peyot* [sidelocks], with his *tzitzit* visible. Curious, the man asked where this young man was from—was he from Poland, Galicia, or Ukraine? He was told: "No, he's from Boston!"

Now, in this country, Bostonians are regarded as being among the most distinguished. . . . So this man was shocked to learn that *even a Bostonian* could look like that—beard, *peyot*, visible *tzitzit*—and yet speak fluent English, and speak with intelligence and clarity about deep concepts like the various levels of Divine unity discussed in the mystical works!

And this had an effect on the observer: First of all, the yeshiva fundraiser who came to visit the town after the young man—he benefited in that this man gave him several extra dollars. But even more significantly, it opened him up to begin making changes in his own life: first in the area of keeping kosher, and gradually in other areas of practical *mitzvah* observance.

And most likely, the young man who set all this in motion has no idea that any of it ever happened!

## IV. SPECTATOR REACTION

It's not only that every event has purpose; the fact that you became aware of it also does. That, too, is by design.

**MYSTIQUE GUST OF KABBALAH IN TZFAT**
Alex Levin (b. 1975), oil on canvas, New York

**TEXT 9**

## Everything Is Providence

The Rebbe, Rabbi Menachem Mendel Schneerson, *Reshimot* #44

"כָּל מַה שֶּׁבָּרָא הַקָּדוֹשׁ בָּרוּךְ הוּא בְּעוֹלָמוֹ, לֹא בָּרָא דָּבָר אֶחָד לְבַטָּלָה" (שַׁבָּת עז, ב) . . . וְכֵן הוּא גַּם כֵּן בְּכָל **הַמְּאוֹרָעוֹת וְהַמִּקְרִים** שֶׁבָּעוֹלָם. שֶׁאֵין דָּבָר אֶחָד לְבַטָּלָה. כִּי הַכֹּל בְּהַשְׁגָּחָה פְּרָטִית . . .

וּבְתוֹר תּוֹצָאָה מִזֶּה: שֶׁאֵין בָּעוֹלָם - **בְּעוֹלָמוֹ שֶׁל כָּל אֶחָד וְאַחַת** אֶלָּא הַשֵּׁם יִתְבָּרֵךְ וְהוּא, כִּי כָּל הַשְּׁאָר, אֵינָם אֶלָּא אֶמְצָעִים, שֶׁעַל יָדָם יִשְׁתַּלֵּם בַּעֲבוֹדָתוֹ לְהַשֵּׁם יִתְבָּרֵךְ.

וְכָל מָה שֶׁאֵינוֹ נוֹגֵעַ לוֹ בַּעֲבוֹדָתוֹ אֶת הַשֵּׁם יִתְבָּרֵךְ, אֵינוֹ יוֹדֵעַ עַל דָּבָר זֶה, **כִּי אֵין דָּבָר וִידִיעָה לְבַטָּלָה, וְכָל הָעוֹלָם כּוּלוֹ - עוֹלָמוֹ הוּא - אֵינוֹ אֶלָּא כְּלִי תַּשְׁמִישׁ וְאֶמְצָעִי, שֶׁעַל יָדוֹ יַגִּיעַ אֶל הַמַּטָּרָה - הַתַּכְלִית שֶׁבִּשְׁבִילָם נִבְרָא.**

"Everything that G-d created in His world [has purpose]; He did not create a single thing in vain" (TALMUD, SHABBAT 77B). . . . The same is also true of all *events and occurrences* in the world: nothing happens in vain. Everything is under Divine providence. . . .

As a result of this: In the world—meaning, *in the personal world of each and every individual*—there exists only G-d and the person. Everything else is merely a means through which the individual fulfills their service of G-d.

Anything that does not pertain to their service of G-d is something they have no awareness of, *for there is no thing or awareness that is in vain. The entire world—one's personal world—is nothing more than a tool and a medium through which they reach their purpose—the ultimate goal for which they were created.*

TEXT 10

## A Lesson in Everything

Rabbi Yisrael Baal Shem Tov, cited in *Hayom Yom*, 9 Iyar

כָּל דָּבָר וְדָבָר אֲשֶׁר הָאָדָם רוֹאֶה אוֹ שׁוֹמֵעַ, הוּא הוֹרָאַת הַנְהָגָה בַּעֲבוֹדַת הַשֵּׁם. וְזֶהוּ עִנְיַן הָעֲבוֹדָה, לְהָבִין וּלְהַשְׂכִּיל מִכָּל דֶּרֶךְ בַּעֲבוֹדַת הַשֵּׁם.

Every single thing one sees or hears is an instruction for their conduct in the service of G-d. This is the idea of *avodah*, service: to comprehend and discern in all things a way in which to serve G-d.

**RABBI YISRAEL BAAL SHEM TOV (BESHT) 1698–1760**

Founder of the Chasidic movement. Born in Okopy, Ukraine, Rabbi Yisrael served as a teacher's assistant before founding the Chasidic movement and revolutionizing the Jewish world with his emphasis on prayer, joy, and love for every Jew, regardless of their level of Torah knowledge. A resident of Mezhibuzh, Ukraine, he was known as the Baal Shem Tov, "master of the good name," for his famous miraculous abilities. The Baal Shem Tov's teachings were written by his students and compiled in *Keter Shem Tov* and other works.

**TEXT 11**

## Seeing No Wrong

Genesis 9:20–23

וַיָּחֶל נֹחַ אִישׁ הָאֲדָמָה וַיִּטַּע כָּרֶם. וַיֵּשְׁתְּ מִן הַיַּיִן
וַיִּשְׁכָּר, וַיִּתְגַּל בְּתוֹךְ אָהֳלֹה. וַיַּרְא חָם אֲבִי כְנַעַן
אֵת עֶרְוַת אָבִיו, וַיַּגֵּד לִשְׁנֵי אֶחָיו בַּחוּץ.

וַיִּקַּח שֵׁם וָיֶפֶת אֶת הַשִּׂמְלָה וַיָּשִׂימוּ עַל שְׁכֶם
שְׁנֵיהֶם וַיֵּלְכוּ אֲחֹרַנִּית, וַיְכַסּוּ אֵת עֶרְוַת אֲבִיהֶם,
וּפְנֵיהֶם אֲחֹרַנִּית וְעֶרְוַת אֲבִיהֶם לֹא רָאוּ.

Noah began to farm and planted a vineyard. He drank from the wine, became drunk, and lay exposed in his tent. Ham, the father of Canaan, saw his father's nakedness and told his two brothers outside.

Shem and Japheth took a garment, laid it across their shoulders, and walked backward to cover their father's nakedness. Their faces were turned away, and they did not see their father's nakedness.

## KEY POINTS

1. When a human artisan forms an object from existing materials, the object exists independently of the artisan. However, when G-d creates something from nothing, it can only exist because G-d is constantly willing it.

2. The principle of Divine providence, as taught by the Baal Shem Tov, means that every single occurrence is specifically guided by G-d—for a reason. G-d doesn't only craft global events. He also scripts every local consequence and does so with intent and purpose.

3. We're not given a checklist to find our purpose, but we are given clues—subtle or obvious—hidden in the flow of daily life. Our mission will always involve doing a *mitzvah*, helping others, or growing personally. The more attuned we are, the more we recognize those Divine cues.

4. Meaning doesn't depend on our ability to see it. Even when we don't understand why something is happening, it still has purpose. Often, we fulfill our mission without ever realizing it—but that doesn't make it any less real.

5 If something enters your awareness, it's part of your mission. That awareness is intentional and meant to guide you. We should see ordinary events not as things that we need to navigate or leverage, but as opportunities packed with personal meaning and purpose.

6 If G-d shows you someone's weakness, it's not so you can gossip or judge—it's so you can help. Your awareness is intentional, and it comes with a responsibility: to support, assist, or guide.

# Stories of Divine Providence

A collection of stories from the sages of the Talmud and the Chasidic masters about Divine providence

### Talmud, Berachot 60b–61a

***Rav Huna said in the name of Rav, who said in the name of Rabbi Meir, and so it was also taught in a Baraita in the name of Rabbi Akiva: A person should always be accustomed to saying, "Everything that G-d does, He does for the best."***

Rabbi Akiva was once traveling along the road. When he reached a certain city he inquired about lodgings, but no one provided him any. Rabbi Akiva said, "Everything that G-d does, He does for the best," and went to sleep in the field.

In Rabbi Akiva's possession were a rooster, a donkey, and a candle. A gust of wind came and extinguished the candle; a cat came and ate the rooster; and a lion came and ate the donkey. Rabbi Akiva said, "Everything that G-d does, He does for the best."

That very night, an army came and captured the city. Rabbi Akiva said, "Did I not tell you? Everything that G-d does, He does for the best."

### Talmud, Taanit 21a

***Nachum Ish Gam Zu was called Gam Zu because, regarding everything that happened to him, he would say, "This, too, is for the good [*gam zu letova*]."***

Once, the Jews wished to send a gift to the court of the emperor. They said, "Who should go and present this gift? Let Nachum Ish Gam Zu go, as he is accustomed to having miracles performed on his behalf." They sent with him a chest filled with precious stones and pearls. On his way, he spent the night at a particular inn. During the night, the residents of the inn arose and took all of the precious jewels and pearls from the chest, and filled it with dirt. The next day, when he saw what had happened, Nachum Ish Gam Zu said, "This, too, is for the good."

When Nachum Ish Gam Zu arrived at the palace, they opened the chest and saw that it was filled with dirt. The emperor, enraged, wanted to kill them all, declaring, "The Jews are mocking me." Nachum Ish Gam Zu said, "This, too, is for the good."

Elijah the Prophet came and appeared before the ruler as one of his officials. He said to the ruler, "Perhaps this dirt is from the earth of their father Abraham. When Abraham threw earth, it turned into swords, and when he threw straw, it turned into arrows, as the verse says, "He made his sword like dirt, his bow like wind-blown straw" (Isaiah 41:2).

There was one city that the Romans had been unable to conquer. They took some of this dirt and tested it by throwing it at their enemies, and they successfully conquered that city. After their victory, the emperor's officers entered the royal treasury and filled Nachum Ish Gam Zu's chest with precious stones and pearls, and sent him off with great honor.

**Based on: The Rebbe, Rabbi Menachem Mendel Schneerson, *Likutei Sichot* 23, p. 468 (February 19, 1979)**

In February 1979, the Chabad's women's organization's midwinter convention was held in suburban Detroit, Michigan. By the time the convention ended, a blizzard on the East Coast grounded all New York-bound flights. The women wrote to the Rebbe, highlighting their stressful situation of being delayed, away from their families, etc. The Rebbe wrote a brief note that was read to the women over the phone. It said:

The Baal Shem Tov's teaching that every occurrence contains a directive in serving G-d is a topic that has been spoken of and discussed at length many, many times; I am sure that you, too, have given speeches on this topic. Yet, now, when an incident has happened to you (i.e., your being delayed in Detroit by the New York snowstorm) whose occurrence has a clear meaning and purpose, you seek to attach to the incident most distorted interpretations (e.g., "Perhaps the delay is designed to distress us," G-d forbid, or "How are we going to return home?" etc.)—anything but the simple and obvious interpretation.

The simple and obvious reason for the delay is: It is possible to disseminate Torah and *mitzvot* to a far greater degree than was accomplished during the Convention. You are therefore being granted the merit—through the snow which descends from Heaven—of completing the above task with an extraordinary abundance and storm intensity of Judaism, similar to the extraordinary abundance of the snowstorm.

Your efforts in completing the Convention's task of disseminating Torah and *mitzvot* should be extended to the city, the airport, publicity in the newspapers, etc.

Of course, the women did just that. They spent the day connecting with fellow Jews, inspiring many of them to added *mitzvah* performance. They returned home the next day.

That evening, after reporting to the Rebbe on the activities of the day, they received an additional reply:

It is a particularly great merit when the A-mighty from On High "points with a finger" and clearly shows one what to DO. May all your activities (undertaken as a result of this Divine indication) be highly successful. It is obvious that each and every woman will soon travel and reach home—for she will have completed her mission.

**Rabbi Yosef Wineberg, "Engine Trouble to the Rescue," Jewish Educational Media, April 11, 2025**

In the early 1950s, I set out on a trip to South Africa to raise funds for the Lubavitcher yeshiva system. Beforehand, I met with the Rebbe.

"Are you stopping anywhere on the way for a day or two?" he asked.

I was flying direct with Pan-American Airlines, but in those days, that still meant making a few refueling stops: in the Azores islands, Portugal, Senegal, Ghana, and Belgian Congo. So I mentioned all of these places to the Rebbe.

"But don't you have to stop on the way for a day or two?" he repeated.

"According to our schedule, we aren't supposed to," was all I could say.

When I came home that day, I told my wife what had happened. "I think I'll end up making a stopover somewhere," I told her. Of course, not knowing where, I just told her not to worry if she doesn't get a telegram that I had safely arrived in South Africa at the expected time.

At the airport in New York, I met a fellow named Mr. Langer, who was also traveling to South Africa to visit his daughter. We had a two-day journey ahead of us, so we were happy to be traveling together.

Around halfway through the trip, we landed in Dakar, Senegal, which was then still a French colony. As we waited for the plane to refuel, I took out a Torah book. I began to study when I noticed a young, dark-skinned man staring at me. I continued what I was doing, but it was quite hot so I took off my hat.

As soon as this man saw my yarmulke underneath, he came over. "There are some French people with beards, so I didn't know whether you are a Jew until you took off your hat," he explained. "I've been living here for six months, and I haven't seen a Jewish face in all that time. I'm so happy to see you now!"

"I come from a place with quite a few Jews, New York," I replied, "but I'm still happy to meet a Jewish man in Dakar."

We began to make conversation, and I learned that his name was Pinto—he was an engineer working for an oil company. He had a wife and two daughters, and had been transferred from his home in Egypt for a job in Senegal.

"Do you have your tefillin?" I queried.

He did—but he did not put them on every day.

"Even a Jew living in Jerusalem has the duty and the privilege of putting on tefillin every day," I told him. "But for a person living here, it is even more crucial. How else will your daughters know that they are Jewish?"

"You've got a point there," he conceded, and he promised to put on tefillin regularly. I was pleased with that, and I headed back to our plane for the next leg, from Dakar to Ghana.

It was meant to be a six-hour flight, but two hours in, we were woken up—there was engine trouble, and we had to turn around. Thank G-d, we managed to land safely in Dakar, but then the pilot came out to inform us that the engine was completely out of order. It would have to be replaced with an entirely new engine that needed to be brought from London—"in no less than forty-eight hours."

The airline took us to a half-decent hotel in the city, and the next morning, after praying, I told Mr. Langer that I was heading out.

"Where are you going?" he protested. "Do you even know French?"

"I don't know French, but the Rebbe asked me twice about stopping along the way. There must be something I'm supposed to do here."

I went out to the street and began asking around, until finally I met a Portuguese man—whose language I could speak.

"Are there any Jews here?" I asked.

The man pointed me to a store just across the street, which belonged to a Jew. I walked in and met the owner's nephew, a young man from Lebanon named Clement Polity.

I ended up spending most of the next two days with Clement. He introduced me to four more Jewish families, while I met another Jewish person at our hotel. Clement arranged a meeting with the locals so that I could speak with them about Judaism, and because he spoke fluent English, he was able to translate into French.

At one point, he turned to me: "Rabbi, I have a personal question. There are no single Jewish girls here; what am I supposed to do?"

I began to explain the importance of marrying within the faith, but I didn't have to work hard. Clement came from a beautiful religious family, and so he understood. He shook hands with me and promised that he would go to France to look for a Jewish girl there.

"Rabbi," he told me before we left, "you will never know what these two days meant for me." By then, our plane had been fixed, and he took me back to the airport.

Afterwards, I wrote a letter to the Rebbe, telling him about this little community and all of the things they needed. Soon after, a package went out from the Rebbe's office with tefillin, as well as some French prayer books and *chumashim*. Then, before Passover, the Rebbe sent them a package of matzah, by airmail, to make sure it arrived on time.

Sometime after Passover, the Rebbe received a letter, signed by both Pinto and Clement. They recounted how, at the community Seder they made—with the Rebbe's matzah—they spoke about how, despite being so busy and so far away, the Rebbe still put in the time and effort to send them tefillin and matzah, without requesting anything in return. This is how a Jew is supposed to behave, they told their children. This letter, which the Rebbe sent on to me, was written with such emotion that it brought tears to my eyes.

That summer, I told the Rebbe that I was going back to South Africa.

"Are you stopping in Dakar?" the Rebbe asked.

"Yes," I answered.

"Even if the plane is in order, you should spend a few days with the families there. But this time, give them notice beforehand."

By then a few more Jewish families had moved there from Egypt, and we learned that the American vice-consul was Jewish, as well. The community got me a room at a beautiful hotel, then came to meet me, and we had a nice farbrengen together.

Everything was fine, except that Clement Polity was still there.

"Clement, you promised me something," I told him when he came to the hotel.

"I kept my promise," he insisted. "I went to France but I didn't find anyone there. But don't you worry—I'll keep trying!"

Six or seven months later, two wedding invitations arrived in the mail—one for the Rebbe and one for me. Clement had found a fine Jewish girl in Lebanon. Later on, he became the chairman of Dakar's Jewish community, and he submitted his name to be published in a local travel guide, along with a notice: "Any Jew who comes to Dakar can call me."

**Rabbi Yisrael Baal Shem Tov, 1698–1760, as related in *Shomer Emunim, Maamar Hashgachah Peratit*, ch. 17**

The Baal Shem Tov was once walking with his students in the field. A strong wind suddenly blew, and a few leaves fell from the tree to the ground. The Baal Shem Tov said to his students: "My children, you should know that the wind that just blew was all for the sake of one worm that was exposed to the sunlight and was suffering from the heat. The worm cried out to G-d, and he sent this wind that blew the leaves down in order to provide shade for this worm."

The Baal Shem Tov concluded, "See how carefully G-d watches over all of His creations, and how great is His mercy for them."

## Psychology References

Sezgin, F., & Erdogan, O., (2015). Academic optimism, hope and zest for work as predictors of teacher self-efficacy and perceived success. *Educational Sciences—Theory & Practice*, vol. 15, no. 1, 7–19.

Hanssen, M. M., et al. (2015). Optimism, motivational coping and well-being: Evidence supporting the importance of flexible goal adjustment. *Journal of Happiness Studies* 16, 1525–1537.

Samios, C., & Baran, S. (2017). Couple adjustment to a stressful life event: A dyadic investigation of the roles of positive reframing and perceived benefits. *Anxiety, Stress, & Coping*, 31(2), 188–205.

Zhou, Y., et al. (2022). The influence of growth mindset on the mental health and life events of college students. *Frontiers in Psychology*, 13, 821206.

Schroder, H. S., et al. (2016). Growth mindsets and psychological distress: A meta-analysis. *Personality and Social Psychology Bulletin*, 42(12), 1608–1622.

Boullion, A., et al. (2021). Mindsets: Investigating resilience. *Personality and Individual Differences*, 174.

AND YOU SHALL CHOOSE LIFE (DEUTERONOMY 30:19) (DETAIL)

Berit Engen, woven tapestry, linen yarn, Oak Park, Illinois, 2008

## I MEAN SOMETHING, THEREFORE I AM

*Before you do anything, you are worthy. Discover Judaism's empowering understanding of your inherent worth as an individual and as a Jew, and how it calls us to even greater achievement.*

## I. MATTERING MATTERS

Throughout this course, we've explored different sources of meaning. Today we focus on one that's often overlooked yet, arguably, most foundational: *mattering*.

**FIRST STEPS**
Nahum Gutman (Russia, 1898–1980, Israel), silkscreen on paper, Israel

**EXERCISE 6.1**

**Who are you? Describe yourself.**

**BITS AND PIECES**
Joshua Meyer, oil on canvas, Cambridge, Massachusetts, 2013

TEXT 1

## The Need to Matter

Zach Mercurio, PhD, "The Science of Mattering: Why Feeling Significant Is So Significant," Medium.com, June 17, 2020

Think about the first time you realized you mattered. What happened? How did you feel?

Chances are your moment of mattering impacted and moved you. Most likely, you felt important because of what *someone else* said or did.

Feeling significant is a basic human desire and a critical factor for mental, emotional, and physical well-being in life, school, and work. . . .

So, what is mattering? Why is mattering so important? And, how can we learn to create the experience of mattering for others? . . .

Researchers find mattering is the feeling that we're a significant part of the world around us: it's the belief that we're *noticed, important,* and *needed*—right now.

While studies show experiencing mattering . . . increases a sense of self-worth and motivation, research also finds it reduces the risk of severe depression, anxiety, and can save lives.

**ZACH MERCURIO, PHD**

Psychology researcher and author. Mercurio earned his PhD in organizational learning, performance, and change from Colorado State University in Fort Collins, Colorado, where he currently serves as a senior fellow researching meaningful work and organization development. He is the author of *The Power of Mattering* and *The Invisible Leader*.

## II. BUILT TO MATTER

Judaism teaches that every person has inherent, categorical value.

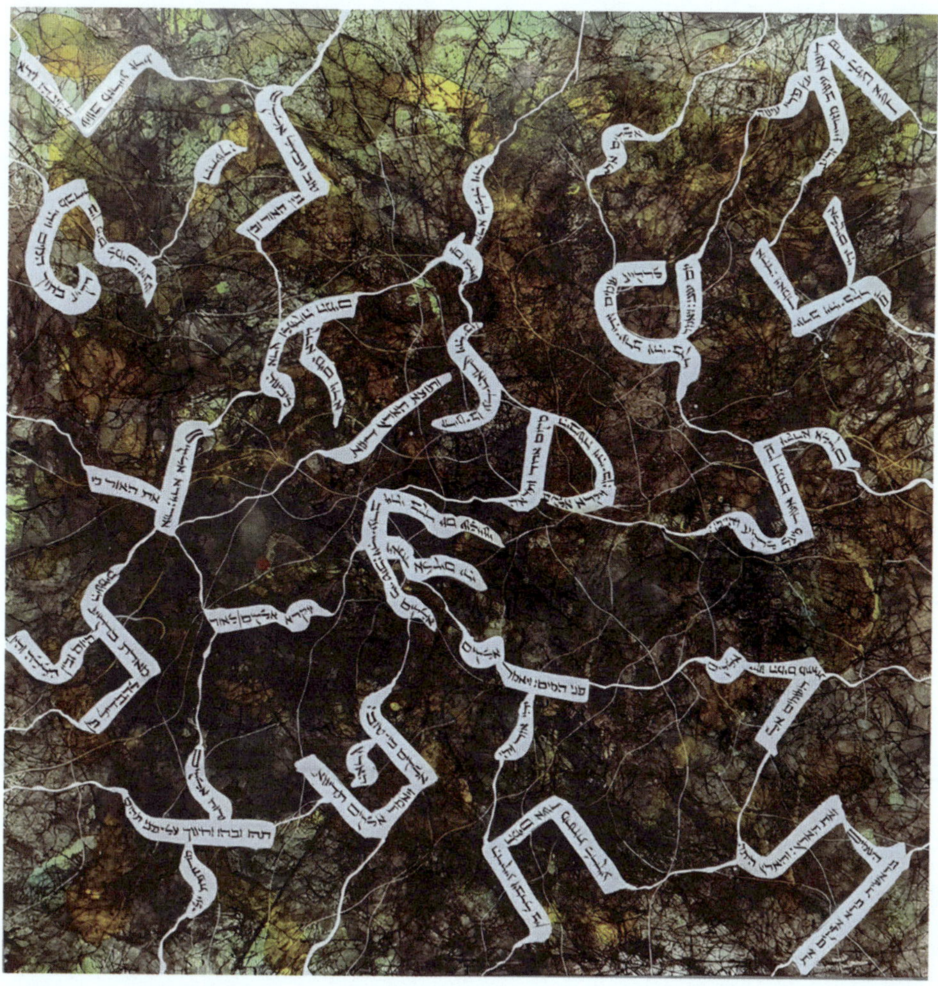

**THE INNER LANGUAGE OF CREATION**

Igal Fedida, mixed material on metal, Israel, 2023

TEXT 2

## "The Craftsman Who Made Me"

Talmud, Taanit 20a–b

מַעֲשֶׂה שֶׁבָּא רַבִּי אֶלְעָזָר בֶּן רַבִּי שִׁמְעוֹן מִמִּגְדַּל גְּדוֹר מִבֵּית רַבּוֹ, וְהָיָה רָכוּב עַל חֲמוֹר וּמְטַיֵּיל עַל שְׂפַת נָהָר, וְשָׂמֵחַ שִׂמְחָה גְדוֹלָה, וְהָיְתָה דַּעְתּוֹ גַּסָּה עָלָיו מִפְּנֵי שֶׁלָּמַד תּוֹרָה הַרְבֵּה.

נִזְדַּמֵּן לוֹ אָדָם אֶחָד שֶׁהָיָה מְכוֹעָר בְּיוֹתֵר. אָמַר לוֹ: "שָׁלוֹם עָלֶיךָ רַבִּי!" וְלֹא הֶחֱזִיר לוֹ.

אָמַר לוֹ: "רֵיקָה, כַּמָּה מְכוֹעָר אוֹתוֹ הָאִישׁ! שֶׁמָּא כָּל בְּנֵי עִירְךָ מְכוֹעָרִין כְּמוֹתְךָ?"

אָמַר לוֹ: "אֵינִי יוֹדֵעַ. אֶלָּא לֵךְ וֶאֱמוֹר לָאוּמָּן שֶׁעֲשָׂאַנִי: 'כַּמָּה מְכוֹעָר כְּלִי זֶה שֶׁעָשִׂיתָ'".

כֵּיוָן שֶׁיָּדַע בְּעַצְמוֹ שֶׁחָטָא, יָרַד מִן הַחֲמוֹר וְנִשְׁתַּטֵּחַ לְפָנָיו, וְאָמַר לוֹ: "נַעֲנֵיתִי לְךָ, מְחוֹל לִי!"

Once, Rabbi Elazar, the son of Rabbi Shimon, was returning from Migdal Gedor, from the home of his teacher. Riding along the riverbank on his donkey, he was feeling proud and content—he had just completed a significant stretch of Torah study.

Along the way, he encountered a man who was unusually unattractive. The man greeted him respectfully: "Peace be upon you, my master!"

**BABYLONIAN TALMUD**

A literary work of monumental proportions that draws upon the legal, spiritual, intellectual, ethical, and historical traditions of Judaism. The 37 tractates of the Babylonian Talmud contain the teachings of the Jewish sages from the period after the destruction of the 2nd Temple through the 5th century CE. It has served as the primary vehicle for the transmission of the Oral Law and the education of Jews over the centuries; it is the entry point for all subsequent legal, ethical, and theological Jewish scholarship.

But Rabbi Elazar did not return the greeting. Instead, he said, “Worthless man! How ugly you are! Are all the people of your town as hideous as you?”

The man replied, “I don’t know. But you should go to the Craftsman who made me and tell Him, ‘How ugly is the vessel You have formed!’”

At once, Rabbi Elazar realized how wrong he had been. He climbed down from his donkey, bowed before the man, and said, “You’ve spoken rightly. I admit my mistake. Please forgive me!”

**TEXT 3**

## G-d’s Image

Mishnah, Avot 3:14

חָבִיב אָדָם שֶׁנִּבְרָא בְּצֶלֶם, חִבָּה יְתֵרָה נוֹדַעַת לוֹ שֶׁנִּבְרָא בְּצֶלֶם, שֶׁנֶּאֱמַר: "כִּי בְּצֶלֶם אֱלֹקִים עָשָׂה אֶת הָאָדָם" (בְּרֵאשִׁית ט, ו).

Human beings are beloved because they were created in the image [of G-d]. They’re even more beloved because G-d let them know that they were created in His image, as it says: “In the image of G-d, He made the human being” (GENESIS 9:6).

**AVOT**
***(ETHICS OF THE FATHERS; PIRKEI AVOT)***

A 6-chapter work on Jewish ethics that is studied widely by Jewish communities, especially during the summer. The first 5 chapters are from the Mishnah, tractate Avot. Avot differs from the rest of the Mishnah in that it does not focus on legal subjects; it is a collection of the sages’ wisdom on topics related to character development, ethics, healthy living, piety, and the study of Torah.

**TEXT 4**

## Unaffected by Creation

Rabbi Shneur Zalman of Liadi, *Likutei Torah*, Megilat Esther 99b

מַהוּתוֹ וְעַצְמוּתוֹ יִתְבָּרֵךְ אֵינוֹ בְּגֶדֶר עָלְמִין כְּלָל, אֲפִילוּ לִהְיוֹת סוֹבֵב וּמְמַלֵּא לְעָלְמִין. כִּי לֹא זֶה הִיא עִיקַר הָאֱלֹקוּת מָה שֶׁהָעוֹלָמוֹת מִתְהַוִּים מִמֶּנּוּ וּמְקַבְּלִים חַיּוּתָם מִמֶּנּוּ יִתְבָּרֵךְ. שֶׁהֲרֵי "אַתָּה הוּא עַד שֶׁלֹּא נִבְרָא הָעוֹלָם וּלְאַחַר שֶׁנִּבְרָא" בְּשָׁוֶה מַמָּשׁ.

וְגַם אִילוּ לֹא הָיָה בּוֹרֵא הָעוֹלָמוֹת, הָיָה הַכֹּל שָׁוֶה לְפָנָיו יִתְבָּרֵךְ.

G-d's essence and being are not defined by the worlds in any way—not even as the One who transcends and fills them. For the essence of G-dliness is not that the worlds were created by Him or receive their life-force from Him. As it is written (SIDDUR, MORNING PRAYERS), "You are [the same] before the world was created and after it was created"—completely unchanged.

Had He not created the worlds, it would have made no difference to Him whatsoever.

**RABBI SHNEUR ZALMAN OF LIADI (ALTER REBBE) 1745–1812**

Chasidic rebbe, Halachic authority, and founder of the Chabad movement. The Alter Rebbe was born in Liozna, Belarus, and was among the principal students of the Magid of Mezeritch. His numerous works include the *Tanya*, an early classic containing the fundamentals of Chabad Chasidism; and *Shulchan Aruch HaRav*, an expanded and reworked code of Jewish law.

**TEXT 5**

## Human Dignity

Rabbi Don Yosef ibn Shoshan, Avot 3:14

חָבִיב אָדָם וְכוּ' חִיבָּה יְתֵירָה וְכוּ'. חוֹבָה עַל כָּל מַשְׂכִּיל לָתֵת אֶל לִבּוֹ כִּי לֹא בָּא רַבִּי עֲקִיבָא עָלָיו הַשָּׁלוֹם לִזְכּוֹר אֵלוּ הַחִיבּוֹת אֶלָּא כְּדֵי לְהָעִיר אֶת הָאָדָם לִהְיוֹת בְּעֵינֵי עַצְמוֹ שֶׁהִיא בְּרִיָּה חֲשׁוּבָה לִפְנֵי מִי שֶׁאָמַר וְהָיָה הָעוֹלָם . . .

רַק יִזָּהֵר אַזְהָרָה יְתֵירָה לָחוּס עַל כְּבוֹד עַצְמוֹ, וּכְבוֹד עַצְמוֹ הוּא כְּבוֹד קוֹנוֹ שֶׁבְּרָאוֹ בְּצֶלֶם וּדְמוּת, וְלֹא יְחַלֵּל אֶת כְּבוֹדוֹ.

"Human beings are beloved . . . even more beloved. . . ." Every thinking person must take this to heart: Rabbi Akiva did not mention these expressions of love just to praise humanity but to awaken a person—to help them recognize that they are a significant being in the eyes of the One who spoke and brought the world into existence.

For this reason, one must be especially careful to protect their own dignity—for that dignity is the dignity of their Creator, who formed them in His image and likeness. To degrade oneself is to degrade Him.

**DON YOSEF IBN SHOSHAN**
**14TH CENTURY**

Kabbalist and ethicist. Born to a prominent Spanish family of Jewish communal leaders and scholars, Don Yosef ibn Shoshan lived in Valencia and Saragossa in the 14th century. He was a Talmudic scholar and a kabbalist, and he is best known for his commentary to *Ethics of the Fathers*, which is cited extensively by later commentators and was published in full in 1968.

TEXT 6

## Created for Me

Mishnah, Sanhedrin 4:5

לְפִיכָךְ נִבְרָא אָדָם יְחִידִי . . . לְפִיכָךְ כָּל אֶחָד וְאֶחָד חַיָּיב לוֹמַר, "בִּשְׁבִילִי נִבְרָא הָעוֹלָם".

Because Adam was created as a single person . . . every individual is required to say, "The world was created just for me."

TEXT 7

## G-d's Children

Mishnah, Avot 3:14

חֲבִיבִין יִשְׂרָאֵל שֶׁנִּקְרְאוּ בָנִים לַמָּקוֹם, חִבָּה יְתֵרָה נוֹדַעַת לָהֶם שֶׁנִּקְרְאוּ בָנִים לַמָּקוֹם, שֶׁנֶּאֱמַר: "בָּנִים אַתֶּם לַה' אֱלֹקֵיכֶם" (דְּבָרִים יד, א)

Beloved are the Jewish people, for they are called children of G-d. An even greater love was shown in that it was made known to them that they are called children of G-d, as it says: "You are children of your G-d" (DEUTERONOMY 14:1).

**MISHNAH**

The first authoritative work of Jewish law that was codified in writing. The Mishnah contains the oral traditions that were passed down from teacher to student; it supplements, clarifies, and systematizes the commandments of the Torah. Due to the continual persecution of the Jewish people, it became increasingly difficult to guarantee that these traditions would not be forgotten. Rabbi Yehudah Hanasi therefore redacted the Mishnah at the end of the 2nd century. It serves as the foundation for the Talmud.

**TEXT 8**

## Part of G-dliness

Rabbi Shneur Zalman of Liadi, *Tanya, Likutei Amarim*, ch. 2

וְנֶפֶשׁ הַשֵּׁנִית בְּיִשְׂרָאֵל הִיא חֵלֶק אֱלוֹ-הַּ מִמַּעַל מַמָּשׁ . . . כְּדִכְתִיב: "בְּנִי בְּכוֹרִי יִשְׂרָאֵל" (שְׁמוֹת ד, כב), "בָּנִים אַתֶּם לַה' אֱלֹקֵיכֶם" (דְּבָרִים יד, א).

פֵּרוּשׁ: כְּמוֹ שֶׁהַבֵּן נִמְשָׁךְ מִמֹּחַ הָאָב, כָּךְ כִּבְיָכוֹל נִשְׁמַת כָּל אִישׁ יִשְׂרָאֵל נִמְשְׁכָה מִמַּחֲשַׁבְתּוֹ וְחָכְמָתוֹ יִתְבָּרֵךְ, דְּאִיהוּ חַכִּים וְלָא בְּחָכְמָה יְדִיעָא, אֶלָּא הוּא וְחָכְמָתוֹ אֶחָד.

The second soul in a Jew is an actual part of G-dliness from above . . . as it says, "Israel is my distinguished and illustrious child" (EXODUS 4:22), and "You are children of your G-d" (DEUTERONOMY 14:1).

Just as a child is drawn from the parents' [essence that is contained in their] mind, so, too, the soul of every Jew is drawn from G-d's wisdom. And since G-d is wise—but not with human, limited wisdom, for He and His wisdom are one—the Jewish soul, which stems from that wisdom, is likewise one with Him.

TEXT 9A

## Beloved Child

Hosea 11:1

כִּי נַעַר יִשְׂרָאֵל וָאֹהֲבֵהוּ, וּמִמִּצְרַיִם קָרָאתִי לִבְנִי.

When Israel was a child, I loved him, and from Egypt I called My son.

**HOSEA**

Biblical book. The book of Hosea is the first part of Trei Asar, a compilation of 12 mini-books, in the Prophets section of the Bible. It contains the prophecies of Hosea, who lived in the 7th century BCE. Hosea's prophesies reprove the Jewish people for their transgressions, warn of Divine consequences, and foretell the Future Redemption.

**CONTRAST**
Raphael Nouril (b. 1940, Iran), oil on canvas

**TEXT 9B**

## Essential Love

The Rebbe, Rabbi Menachem Mendel Schneerson, *Likutei Sichot* 21, p. 20

אַ בֵּן גָדוֹל, וָואס אִיז שׁוֹין אוֹיסְגֶעוַואקְסְן בְּשֵׂכֶל וּמִדּוֹת וְכוּ' - אִיז דִי אַהֲבַת הָאָב אֵלָיו נִיט אַלֶעמָאל נָאר מִצַד דֶעם אַלֵיין וָואס עֶר אִיז זַיין קִינְד. דֶער אָב קֶען עֶם אוֹיךְ לִיבְּ הָאבֶּען וַוייל דֶער בֶּן אִיז אַ חָכָם אוּן פִירְט זִיךְ עַל פִּי שֵׂכֶל, וַוייל עֶר הָאט מִדּוֹת טוֹבוֹת, אָדֶער וַוייל דֶער בֶּן אִיז שְׁטַארְק זָהִיר אִין כִּיבּוּד אָב. וָואס דָאס אַלְץ אִיז אַן אַהֲבָה וָואס אִיז מִצַד הַטַעַם.

מָה שֶׁאֵין כֵּן דִי אַהֲבָה פוּן אַ פָּאטֶער צוּ אַ בֵּן קָטָן, אִיז . . . נִיט מִצַד (הַטַעַם -) מַעֲלַת בְּנוֹ, נָאר זִי אִיז אַן אַהֲבָה עַצְמִית: וִויבַּאלְד אַז עֶר אִיז זַיין קִינְד, וָואס אָב וּבֵן זַיינֶען עֶצֶם אֶחָד, דֶערִיבֶּער הָאט עֶר אִים לִיבְּ.

בַּיי אַ בֵּן גָדוֹל, אַף עַל פִּי וָואס אוֹיךְ עֶר אִיז עֶצֶם אֶחָד מִיט אָבִיו, וִויבַּאלְד אָבֶּער אַז סְ'אִיז דָא אוֹיךְ אַן אַהֲבָה שֶׁעַל פִּי טַעַם, פַארְדֶעקְט זִי אוֹיף דֶער אַהֲבָה עַצְמִית וָואס אִיז דָא צְוִוישְׁן זֵיי.

A father's love for an older child, who has developed intellect and refined character, may not come solely from the fact that this is the father's child. It may also be because the child is wise, well-mannered, or respectful—and that's love rooted in reason.

**RABBI MENACHEM MENDEL SCHNEERSON 1902–1994**

The towering Jewish leader of the 20th century, known as "the Lubavitcher Rebbe," or simply as "the Rebbe." Born in southern Ukraine, the Rebbe escaped Nazi-occupied Europe, arriving in the U.S. in June 1941. The Rebbe inspired and guided the revival of traditional Judaism after the European devastation, impacting virtually every Jewish community the world over. The Rebbe often emphasized that the performance of just one additional good deed could usher in the era of Mashiach. The Rebbe's scholarly talks and writings have been printed in more than 200 volumes.

But a father's love for a young child is different. It's not about what the child does or doesn't do. It's an essential love—because they are one. Father and child are of one essence.

With an older child, though this essential bond remains, the love that stems from observable qualities can sometimes overshadow it. The essential love is always there—it's just not always on display.

TEXT 10

## No Choice

Midrash, *Ruth Rabah, Petichta* 3

בְּאוֹתָהּ שָׁעָה אָמַר הַקָּדוֹשׁ בָּרוּךְ הוּא:

"בְּנֵי סַרְבָנִין הֵן! לְכַלוֹתָן אִי אֶפְשָׁר, לְהַחֲזִירָן לְמִצְרַיִם אִי אֶפְשָׁר, לְהַחְלִיפָם בְּאוּמָּה אַחֶרֶת אֵינִי יָכוֹל".

At that time, G-d said:

"My children are stubborn [but what shall I do]? To destroy them? That is impossible. To have them return to Egypt? That is impossible. To exchange them for another nation? I simply cannot."

***RUTH RABAH***

A Midrashic text on the book of Ruth. *Midrash* is the designation of a particular genre of rabbinic literature. The term Midrash is derived from the root *d-r-sh* (*dalet-resh-shin*), which means "to search," "to examine," and "to investigate." This particular Midrash provides textual exegeses, expounds upon the biblical narrative of Ruth, and develops and illustrates moral principles. It was first printed in Pesaro, Italy, in 1519, together with four other Midrashic works on the other four biblical *megilot*.

## III. ROYAL PRIVILEGE

Being created in G-d's image with inherent value is not just a privilege; it is a responsibility to conduct ourselves in a G-dly manner.

**EVENING PRAYER (DETAIL)**
Alphonse Levy (1843–1918), Musée d'Art et d'Histoire du Judaïsme, Paris, 1883

QUESTION

**If we already matter unconditionally, why strive, grow, or change at all?**

TEXT 11

## The *Mitzvah* of Self-Care

Midrash, *Vayikra Rabah* 34:3

"גֹּמֵל נַפְשׁוֹ אִישׁ חָסֶד" (מִשְׁלֵי יא, יז) - זֶה הִלֵּל הַזָּקֵן.

שֶׁבְּשָׁעָה שֶׁהָיָה נִפְטָר מִתַּלְמִידָיו הָיָה מְהַלֵּךְ וְהוֹלֵךְ
עִמָּם, אָמְרוּ לוֹ תַּלְמִידָיו: "רַבֵּנוּ! לְהֵיכָן אַתָּה הוֹלֵךְ?"

אָמַר לָהֶם: "לַעֲשׂוֹת מִצְוָה".

אָמְרוּ לוֹ: "וְכִי מַה מִּצְוָה זוֹ?"

אָמַר לָהֶן: "לִרְחֹץ בְּבֵית הַמֶּרְחָץ".

אָמְרוּ לוֹ: "וְכִי זוֹ מִצְוָה הִיא?"

אָמַר לָהֶם: "הֵן! מָה אִם אִיקוֹנִין שֶׁל מְלָכִים שֶׁמַּעֲמִידִים
אוֹתָן בְּבָתֵּי טַרְטִיאוֹת וּבְבָתֵּי קִרְקָסִיאוֹת, מִי שֶׁנִּתְמַנֶּה
עֲלֵיהֶם הוּא מוֹרְקָן וְשׁוֹטְפָן וְהֵן מַעֲלִין לוֹ מְזוֹנוֹת,
וְלֹא עוֹד אֶלָּא שֶׁהוּא מִתְגַּדֵּל עִם גְּדוֹלֵי מַלְכוּת,

אֲנִי שֶׁנִּבְרֵאתִי בְּצֶלֶם וּבִדְמוּת, דִּכְתִיב, 'כִּי בְּצֶלֶם אֱלֹקִים
עָשָׂה אֶת הָאָדָם' (בְּרֵאשִׁית ט, ו), עַל אַחַת כַּמָּה וְכַמָּה!"

"A kind person benefits their own soul" (PROVERBS 11:17)—this refers to Hillel the Elder.

***VAYIKRA RABAH***

An early rabbinic commentary on the book of Leviticus. This Midrash, written in Aramaic and Hebrew, provides textual exegeses and anecdotes, expounds upon the biblical narrative, and develops and illustrates moral principles. It was first printed in Constantinople in 1512 together with 4 other Midrashic works on the other 4 books of the Pentateuch.

When Hillel would part ways with his students, he would continue walking with them. They once asked him, "Rebbe, where are you going?"

He replied, "To fulfill a *mitzvah*."

"What *mitzvah*?" they asked.

"To bathe in the bathhouse," he said.

"Is that really a *mitzvah*?" they wondered aloud.

He said, "Of course. Think about it: Statues of kings are placed in theaters and stadiums. The officials appointed to care for them wash and polish them regularly. They get paid for it, and they're honored for it—they move in the circles of nobility.

"[Now if that's how we treat lifeless images made in honor of human kings] how much more so with me, a human being who was fashioned in the Divine image and likeness, as it is written: 'For in the image of G-d He made the human being' (GENESIS 9:6)!"

TEXT 12A

## Honoring G-d

Talmud, Shabbat 50b

דְתַנְיָא: רוֹחֵץ אָדָם פָּנָיו יָדָיו וְרַגְלָיו בְּכָל יוֹם בִּשְׁבִיל קוֹנוֹ, מִשּׁוּם שֶׁנֶּאֱמַר: "כֹּל פָּעַל ה' לַמַּעֲנֵהוּ" (מִשְׁלֵי טז, ד).

It was taught: a person should wash their face, hands, and feet each day in honor of their Creator, as it is written: "Everything G-d made, He made for His own sake" (PROVERBS 16:4).

TEXT 12B

## Honoring G-d

Rashi, ad loc.

**בִּשְׁבִיל קוֹנֵהוּ** - לִכְבוֹד קוֹנֵהוּ. דִכְתִיב, "כִּי בְּצֶלֶם אֱלֹקִים עָשָׂה וְגוֹ'".

וְעוֹד דְהָרוֹאֶה בְּרִיּוֹת נָאוֹת אוֹמֵר, "בָּרוּךְ שֶׁכָּכָה לוֹ בְּעוֹלָמוֹ!"

"In honor of their Creator": meaning, to honor the One Who made them, as it says, "For in the image of G-d He made the human being."

And when others see a beautiful person, they're inspired to say, "Blessed is the One Who has such beauty in His world!"

**RABBI SHLOMO YITZCHAKI (RASHI) 1040–1105**

Most noted biblical and Talmudic commentator. Born in Troyes, France, Rashi studied in the famed *yeshivot* of Mainz and Worms. His commentaries on the Pentateuch and the Talmud, which focus on the straightforward meaning of the text, appear in virtually every edition of the Talmud and Bible.

TEXT 13A

## Children's Responsibilities

Deuteronomy 14:1–3

בָּנִים אַתֶּם לַה' אֱלֹקֵיכֶם. לֹא תִתְגֹּדְדוּ וְלֹא תָשִׂימוּ קָרְחָה בֵּין עֵינֵיכֶם לָמֵת.

כִּי עַם קָדוֹשׁ אַתָּה לַה' אֱלֹקֶיךָ, וּבְךָ בָּחַר ה' לִהְיוֹת לוֹ לְעַם סְגֻלָּה מִכֹּל הָעַמִּים אֲשֶׁר עַל פְּנֵי הָאֲדָמָה.

לֹא תֹאכַל כָּל תּוֹעֵבָה.

You are children of your G-d. Do not cut yourselves nor tear out the hair of your head for the dead.

For you are a holy people to your G-d, and He has chosen you to be His treasured people from among all the nations on the face of the earth.

Do not eat any detestable thing.

TEXT 13B

## Children's Responsibilities

Rashi, ad loc.

**לֹא תִתְגֹּדְדוּ.** לֹא תִתְּנוּ גְדִידָה וְשֶׂרֶט בִּבְשַׂרְכֶם עַל מֵת כְּדֶרֶךְ שֶׁהָאֱמוֹרִיִּים עוֹשִׂין. לְפִי שֶׁאַתֶּם בָּנָיו שֶׁל מָקוֹם, וְאַתֶּם רְאוּיִין לִהְיוֹת נָאִים, וְלֹא גְדוּדִים וּמְקֹרָחִים.

"Do not cut yourselves": Do not make cuts or incisions in your flesh to mourn for the dead, as the Amorites do. Because you are the children of G-d, it is appropriate for you to be dignified and handsome and not wounded or with your hair torn out.

TEXT 14

## Royal Reminder

Talmud, Zevachim 19a

אָמַר רַב אָשֵׁי, אָמַר לִי הוּנָא בַּר נָתָן: זִימְנָא חֲדָא הֲוָה קָאִימְנָא קַמֵּיהּ דְאִיזְגַּדַר מַלְכָּא וַהֲוָה מִדְלֵי לִי הֶמְיָינַאי, וְתַיְתְיֵיהּ נִיהֲלֵיהּ, וְאָמַר לִי: "מַמְלֶכֶת כֹּהֲנִים וְגוֹי קָדוֹשׁ" (שְׁמוֹת יט, ו) כְּתִיב בְּכוּ.

Rav Ashi says: Huna bar Natan once told me: "I was once standing before King Izgadar of Persia, and my belt had slipped too high. The king personally adjusted it back in place and said to me, 'A kingdom of priests and a holy nation' (EXODUS 19:6)—that's what is written about you."

## IV. WHAT WILL YOU DO WITH IT?

Being G‑d's child means your worth is constant and unshakable. But that very worth makes your choices matter: your actions carry weight because you matter.

**KEDOSHIM (HOLY ONES)**
Yoram Raanan, acrylic on canvas, Israel, 2014

**TEXT 15**

## Divine Alignment

The Rebbe, Rabbi Menachem Mendel Schneerson,
*Likutei Sichot* 21, pp. 23–25

זַייֶענְדִיק בְּנוֹ שֶׁל הַקָדוֹשׁ בָּרוּךְ הוּא – דֶער עֶצֶם פוּן אִידְן אִיז אֵיין זַאךְ מִיט אֱלוֹקוּת – בְּרֵיינְגְט דָאס מִמֵילָא אַז אַלֶע עִנְיָנֵי הָאָדָם זַיינֶען אֵיינְס מִיט אֱלוֹקוּת, זַיין שֵׂכֶל אִיז צוּ לֶערְנֶען תּוֹרָה, זַיינֶע מִדוֹת אוֹיף אַהֲבַת הַשֵׁם אוּן יִרְאַת הַשֵׁם.

Being a child of G-d—meaning that the essence of a Jew is united with G-dliness—naturally brings about a state in which every part of the person is also aligned with G-dliness: the mind is drawn to Torah study, and the emotional character is directed toward love and awe of G-d.

## V. THE END IS THE BEGINNING

The six lessons of this course all come down to a single truth: Meaning isn't something you chase. It's something you carry. Ultimately, the Jewish view of a meaningful life is not the search for mattering but the expression of it.

**SOLDIER AT PRAYER**
Sam Griffin, oil on canvas, Israel, 2025

**EXERCISE 6.2**

**Complete the following sentence:**

**"Because I matter, today I will ________________________"**

**YOUNG HAPPY FAMILY**
Izik Fleishiker (b. 1957), oil on canvas, Israel, Safrai Gallery, Jerusalem

## KEY POINTS

1. Judaism teaches that every person has inherent, categorical value. Our value doesn't start with what we've done but with the simple fact that we were created by G-d, with intent and purpose.

2. Every person has inherent worth simply by virtue of existing—mirroring G-d, Whose value stems from His essence, not from what He does. This value is individual, not based on group identity, as reflected in the creation of Adam as a single human being.

3. The Jewish people are referred to as G-d's "children." Just as a parent's love for their child is constant and unconditional, G-d's love for us remains firm regardless of our actions. He wants us to know we are His children so that this truth shapes our self-perception.

4. Being created in the image of G-d is a responsibility. It requires us to ensure that we act accordingly by caring for ourselves physically and emulating G-d's conduct.

5. As G-d's children, our worth is constant and unshakable. But that very worth makes our choices matter: our actions carry weight because we matter. Being G-d's children should naturally inspire us to devotion to G-d's causes.

# Respecting Human Dignity

*Kavod haberiyot*, respect for human dignity, is a key principle in Jewish thought and law. The following texts explore this principle and its ramifications.

## THE PRINCIPLE

Mishnah, Avot 4:1

**Who is honorable? One who honors his fellows. As the verse states, "For to those who honor me, I accord honor; those who scorn me shall be demeaned" (I Samuel 2:30).**

Midrash, *Bereshit Rabah* 24:7

**Rabbi Akiva said: The verse "Love your fellow as yourself" (Leviticus 19:18) is a fundamental principle in the Torah. Don't say, "Since I was insulted, my friend should be insulted together with me," or "Since I was cursed, let my friend be cursed together with me."**

**Rabbi Tanchuma said: If you act this way, know who you're really disrespecting—for your fellow human was made in the image of G-d.**

Rabbi Moshe Cordovero, *Tomer Devorah*, ch. 2

**A person should train themselves in two habits:**

**First, to honor every created being. When you reflect on the greatness of the Creator Who made each person with wisdom—and not just people, but all creatures—you will come to see how tremendously valuable each one is. After all, the exalted and all-wise Creator invested His wisdom into making every being. To insult them, then, is to insult their Creator.**

**Imagine an artisan who crafts an object with great skill and then displays it. If someone came along and mocked the piece, how offensive would that be to its creator? By mocking the object they have created, they are mocking the abilities of the craftsperson behind it.**

**In the same way, G-d is displeased when any of His creations are scorned. As the verse says, "How masterful are Your works, O G-d" (Psalms 104:24). The verse uses the Hebrew word *rabu*, which connotes "masterful," not only "great." The verse continues, "You made them all with wisdom." Since G-d invested His wisdom in His creations, they are great and masterful. Therefore, we should reflect on G-d's creations and appreciate the wisdom in them—not treat them with contempt.**

**Second, you should develop genuine love in your heart for other humans—even for those who are wicked. Think of them as your siblings—or even closer than that—until love for all people becomes deeply rooted in your heart. You should love even the wicked and think to yourself, "If only they would return to G-d and become righteous: great and pleasing to G-d." This was the attitude of Moses, who said, "If only all of G-d's people were prophets!" (Numbers 11:29).**

**How can you cultivate this kind of love? Focus your thoughts on their positive traits. Overlook their flaws. Don't fixate on their failings—focus instead on their strengths.**

## BIBLICAL EXAMPLES

Exodus 21:37

**If a person steals an ox or a sheep and slaughters it or sells it, they must pay back five head of cattle for the ox and four sheep for the sheep.**

*Mechilta*, Mishpatim 12

**Rabbi Yochanan ben Zakkai says: G-d is concerned for the dignity of His creations.**

**This is why when someone steals an ox—an animal that walks on its own—the thief must repay five times its value.**

**But if someone steals a sheep—which the thief typically carries on their shoulders [thereby embarrassing themselves]—they repay only four times its value.**

## LEGAL PRINCIPLE

Maimonides, *Mishneh Torah*, Laws of Forbidden Mixtures 1:29

**When a person sees their fellow wearing clothing containing a mixture [of wool and linen] that is forbidden by Torah law, they should jump up and rip it off them immediately—even if the person is walking in the marketplace. This applies even to one's teacher.**

**For the obligation to respect human dignity does not supersede a negative prohibition in the Torah. . . .**

**However, a prohibition is that is rabbinic in origin is superseded by human dignity in all situations. Although the Torah states "Do not deviate from any of the statements the sages relate to you" (Deuteronomy 17:11), this prohibition is superseded by considerations of a human dignity.**

**Accordingly, if a person is wearing a mixture that is only forbidden by rabbinic decree, one may not rip it off him in the marketplace, nor must the person themself remove it in the marketplace before they arrive home.**

## Psychology References

George, L. S., & Park, C. L. (2016). Meaning in life as comprehension, purpose, and mattering: Toward integration and new research questions. *Review of General Psychology,* 20(3), 205–220.

Schieman, S., & Taylor, J. (2001). Statuses, roles, and the sense of mattering. *Sociological Perspectives*, 44(4), 469–484.

Neff, K. (2011). Self-compassion, self-esteem, and well-being. *Social and Personality Psychology Compass*, vol. 5, issue 1, Jan. 2011.

Neff, K. (2023) Self-compassion: Theory, method, research, and intervention. *Annual Review of Psychology*, vol. 74:193–218, 2023.

Grubbs, J. B., & Exline, J. J. (2016). Trait entitlement: A cognitive-personality source of vulnerability to psychological distress. *Psychological Bulletin,* 142(11), 1168–1188.

Brown, A., & Dutton, K. A. (2015). The positive impact of trait self-esteem on daily happiness: Evidence from experience sampling. *Personality and Individual Differences,* 85, 26–31.

## Acknowledgments

We are grateful to the following individuals for their contributions to this course:

*Flagship Director*

**RABBI SHMULY KARP**

*Curriculum Coordinator*

**RIVKI MOCKIN**

*Flagship Administrator*

**NAOMI HEBER**

*Editor*

**RABBI NAFTALI SILBERBERG**

*Curriculum Team*

**RABBI LAZER GURKOV**
**RABBI YOCHANAN RIVKIN**
**RABBI SHMUEL SUPER**

*Instructor Advisory Board*

**RABBI YOSEF LEVIN**
**RABBI LEVI GREENBERG**
**RABBI SENDER GEISINSKY**
**RABBI YISRAEL RICE**
**RABBI ZUSHE RIVKIN**

*Research*

**RABBI YAKOV GERSHON**

*Copywriter*

**RABBI YONI BROWN**

*Proofreading*

**RACHEL MUSICANTE**
**YA'AKOVAH WEBER**

*Hebrew Punctuation*

**RABBI MOSHE WOLFF**

*Continuing Education*

**SHULAMIS NADLER**
**MINDY WALLACH**

*Instructor Support*

**RABBI SHOLOM BAITELMAN**
**RABBI TZALY DUBOV**
**RABBI LEVI GOLDSHMID**
**RABBI AVREMI RAPOPORT**

*Design and Layout Administrator*

**SARA OSDOBA**

*Textbook and Marketing Design*

**LEAH FAINZILBER**
**CHAYA MUSHKA KANNER**
**CHAYA KATZ**
**ESTIE KLEIN**
**RABBI LEVI WEINGARTEN**

*Textbook Layout*

**RABBI MOTTI KLEIN**

*Imagery*

**CHAYA BARNETT**
**SARA ROSENBLUM**

*Permissions*

**ESTY DONIN**
**SHULAMIS NADLER**

*Publication and Distribution*

**RABBI MOSHE RAICHIK**
**RABBI MENDEL SIROTA**

*PowerPoint Presentations*

**CHAYA BARNETT**
**SARA ROSENBLUM**

*Course Videos*

**GETZY RASKIN**
**MOSHE RASKIN**

*Key Points Videos*

**RABBI AVREMI RAPOPORT**

**Rabbi Moshe Kotlarsky**, *z"l*, our beloved mentor, friend, and JLI chairman, was the visionary who saw the potential of JLI from its very inception, wholeheartedly supporting and shepherding its growth and expansion, along with the countless other Chabad programs and services he directed across the globe. May the merit of the Torah study by JLI students worldwide serve to honor Rabbi Kotlarsky's legacy, continuing to be a source of *nachas* to him on high, as it always was during his lifetime.

Thanks to Rabbi Kotlarsky, we are fortunate to have the unwavering support of JLI's principal benefactor, **Mr. George Rohr**, who is fully invested in our work, continues to be instrumental to JLI's monumental growth, and is largely responsible for the Jewish renaissance that is being spearheaded by JLI and its affiliates worldwide.

The commitment and sage direction of JLI's dedicated Executive Board—**Rabbis Chaim Block**, **Hesh Epstein**, **Ronnie Fine**, **Yosef Gansburg**, **Shmuel Kaplan**, **Yisrael Rice**, and **Avrohom Sternberg**—and the countless hours they devote to the development of JLI are what drive the vision, growth, and tremendous success of the organization.

Finally, JLI represents an incredible partnership of more than 1,600 *shluchim* and *shluchot* in more than 1,000 locations across the globe who contribute their time and talent to furthering Jewish adult education. We thank them for generously sharing feedback and making suggestions that steer JLI's development and growth. They are our most valuable critics and our most cherished contributors.

Inspired by the call of the **Lubavitcher Rebbe**, of righteous memory, it is the mandate of the Rohr JLI to provide a community of learning for all Jews throughout the world where they can participate in their precious heritage of Torah study and experience its rewards. May this course succeed in fulfilling this sacred charge!

On behalf of the Rohr Jewish Learning Institute,

**RABBI EFRAIM MINTZ**
*Executive Director*

Rosh Chodesh Elul, 5785

## The Rohr Jewish Learning Institute

**AN AFFILIATE OF MERKOS L'INYONEI CHINUCH,**
**THE EDUCATION ARM OF THE CHABAD-LUBAVITCH MOVEMENT**
832 EASTERN PARKWAY, BROOKLYN, NY 11213

#### CURRICULUM DEVELOPMENT

*Rabbi Mordechai Dinerman*
*Rabbi Naftali Silberberg*
EDITORS IN CHIEF

*Rabbi Shmuel Klatzkin, PhD*
ACADEMIC CONSULTANT

*Rabbi Eli Block*
*Rabbi Yoni Brown*
*Rabbi Mendy Goldberg*
*Rabbi Eliezer Gurkow*
*Rabbi Meir Kerzner*
*Rabbi Berel Polityko*
*Rabbi Schneur Pruss*
*Rabbi Yochanan Rivkin*
*Rabbi Levi Shmotkin*
*Rabbi Shmuel Super*
CURRICULUM AUTHORS

*Rabbi Ahrele Loschak*
EDITOR, TORAH STUDIES

*Rabbi Yaakov Paley*
WRITER

*Rabbi Moshe Wolff*
EDITORIAL SUPPORT

*Rabbi Yakov Gershon*
RESEARCH

*Rabbi Michoel Lipskier*
EXPERIENTIAL LEARNING

*Mrs. Rivki Mockin*
CONTENT COORDINATOR

#### MARKETING AND BRANDING

*Yonatan Azrielant*
*Yosef Feigelstock*
*Sholom Gurary*
*Rochel Horowitz*
*Schneur Pruss*
*Avremi Rapoport*
*Shabi Soffer*
MARKETING AND SOCIAL MEDIA

*Ms. Sara Osdoba*
DESIGN ADMINISTRATOR

*Ms. Kelly Broyn*
*Ms. Leah Fainzilber*
*Mrs. Chaya Mushka Kanner*
*Mrs. Chaya Katz*
*Mrs. Estie Klein*
*Rabbi Levi Weingarten*
GRAPHIC DESIGN

*Rabbi Sholom Gurary*
*Rabbi Motti Klein*
*Rabbi Zalman Korf*
*Rabbi Moshe Wolff*
PUBLICATION DESIGN

*Rabbi Yaakov Paley*
COPYWRITER

*Rabbi Yossi Grossbaum*
*Rabbi Mendel Lifshitz*
*Rabbi Shraga Sherman*
*Rabbi Ari Sollish*
*Rabbi Mendel Teldon*
MARKETING COMMITTEE

#### MARKETING CONSULTANTS

*Alan Rosenspan*
ALAN ROSENSPAN & ASSOCIATES
Sharon, MA

*Gary Wexler*
PASSION MARKETING
Los Angeles, CA

#### JLI CENTRAL

*Rabbi Sholom Baitelman*
*Mrs. Mimi Brawer*
*Ms. Chanie Chesney*
*Rabbi Tzali Dubov*
*Ms. Kayla Fogelman*
*Rabbi Levi Goldshmid*
*Ms. Mushka Majeski*
*Rabbi Avremi Rapoport*
*Mrs. Aliza Scheinfeld*
*Ms. Mushka Silberstein*
*Rabbi Yosef Vogel*
*Ms. Mimi Wilhelm*
ADMINISTRATION

*Mrs. Hannah Ginsburg*
*Ms. Liba Leah Gutnick*
*Rabbi Motti Klein*
*Mrs. Chana Marasow*
*Mrs. Rochel Perlstein*
*Rabbi Shlomie Tenenbaum*
PROJECT MANAGERS

*Mrs. Mindy Wallach*
AFFILIATE ORIENTATION

*Ms. Chaya Barnett*
*Mrs. Tova Cohen*
*Rabbi Motti Klein*
*Ms. Leah Lipskier*
*Getzy Raskin*
*Moshe Raskin*
*Mrs. Sara Rosenblum*
MULTIMEDIA DEVELOPMENT

*Rabbi Mendel Ashkenazi*
*Yoni Ben-Oni*
*Rabbi Mendy Elishevitz*
*Rabbi Yirmi Emmer*
*Mendel Grossbaum*
*Rabbi Aron Liberow*
*Mrs. Chana Weinbaum*
ONLINE DIVISION

*Mrs. Ya'akovah Weber*
SENIOR PROOFREADER & COPY EDITOR

*Mrs. Rachel Musicante*
*Ms. Chaya Barnett*
PROOFREADERS

*Rabbi Moshe Raichik*
*Rabbi Mendel Sirota*
PRINTING AND DISTRIBUTION

*Ms. Esty Donin*
*Mrs. Shaina B. Mintz*
*Mrs. Shulamis Nadler*
*Ms. Chinkah Zirkind*
ACCOUNTING

*Mrs. Tova Cohen*
*Mrs. Shulamis Nadler*
*Mrs. Mindy Wallach*
*Mrs. Mimi Wilhelm*
CONTINUING EDUCATION

#### JLI FLAGSHIP

*Rabbi Yisrael Rice*
CHAIRMAN

*Rabbi Shmuly Karp*
DIRECTOR

*Mrs. Naomi Heber*
ADMINISTRATOR

#### PAST FLAGSHIP AUTHORS

*Rabbi Yitzchak M. Kagan*
of blessed memory

*Rabbi Zalman Abraham*
Brooklyn, NY

*Rabbi Berel Bell*
Montreal, QC

*Rabbi Nissan D. Dubov*
London, UK

*Rabbi Tzvi Freeman*
Atlanta, GA

*Rabbi Eliezer Gurkow*
London, ON

*Rabbi Aaron Herman*
Pittsburgh, PA

*Rabbi Simon Jacobson*
New York, NY

*Rabbi Chaim D. Kagan, PhD*
Monsey, NY

*Rabbi Shmuel Klatzkin, PhD*
Dayton, OH

*Rabbi Nochum Mangel*
Dayton, OH

*Rabbi Moshe Miller, OBM*
Chicago, IL

*Rabbi Yosef Paltiel*
Brooklyn, NY

*Rabbi Yehuda Pink*
Solihull, UK

*Rabbi Yisrael Rice*
S. Rafael, CA

*Rabbi Eli Silberstein*
Ithaca, NY

*Mrs. Rivkah Slonim*
Binghamton, NY

*Rabbi Avrohom Sternberg*
New London, CT

*Rabbi Shais Taub*
Cedarhurst, NY

*Rabbi Shlomo Yaffe*
Longmeadow, MA

### ROSH CHODESH SOCIETY

*Rabbi Shmuel Kaplan*
CHAIRMAN

*Mrs. Shaindy Jacobson*
DIRECTOR

*Mrs. Chana Dechter*
ADMINISTRATOR

*Mrs. Malky Bitton*
*Mrs. Shula Bryski*
*Mrs. Rochel Holzkenner*
*Mrs. Leah Rosenfeld*
*Mrs. Yehudis Wolvovsky*
EDITORIAL BOARD

### TORAH STUDIES

*Rabbi Yosef Gansburg*
CHAIRMAN

*Rabbi Shlomie Tenenbaum*
ADMINISTRATOR

*Rabbi Ahrele Loschak*
EDITOR

*Rabbi Lazer Gurkow*
CONTRIBUTING AUTHOR

*Rabbi Levi Fogelman*
*Rabbi Yaacov Halperin*
*Rabbi Nechemia Schusterman*
*Rabbi Ari Sollish*
STEERING COMMITTEE

### JLI TEENS

*In Partnership with CTeen: Chabad Teen Network*

*Rabbi Chaim Block*
CHAIRMAN

*Rabbi Shlomie Tenenbaum*
ADMINISTRATOR

### THE GOLDSTEIN FELLOWSHIP

*Edwin and Arlene Goldstein*
FOUNDERS AND PATRONS

*Rabbi Shlomie Tenenbaum*
PROGRAM COORDINATOR

*Mrs. Mindy Wallach*
ACCREDITATION

*Hannah Ginsburg*
*Liba Leah Gutnick*
*Rochel Perlstein*
ADMINISTRATION

### SINAI SCHOLARS SOCIETY

*In Partnership with Chabad on Campus*

*Rabbi Dubi Rabinowitz*
DIRECTOR

*Rabbi Levi Goldshmid*
MANAGING DIRECTOR

*Rabbi Avin Kreisler*
VAYAKRI CLUB

*Ms. Yocheved Batyah Michelashvili*
*Mrs. Mussi Schneerson*
*Mrs. Manya Sperlin*
*Mrs. Mimi Wilhelm*
TEAM MEMBERS

*Mrs. Devorah Zlatopolsky*
SHLUCHIM AND STUDENT LIAISON

*Rabbi Chaim Leib Hilel*
*Rabbi Yossi Lazaroff*
*Rabbi Aryeh Schwartz*
*Rabbi Shmuel Tiechtel*
*Rabbi Didy Waks*

*Rabbi Shmuly Weiss*
STEERING COMMITTEE

### THE WELLNESS INSTITUTE

*Rabbi Efraim Mintz*
EXECUTIVE DIRECTOR
THE JEWISH LEARNING INSTITUTE

*Rabbi Zalman Abraham*
DIRECTOR

*Sara Weiss*
ADMINISTRATOR

*Pamela Dubin*
IMPACT ANALYSIS

*Mindy Wallach*
CONTINUING EDUCATION ADMINISTRATOR

*Dina Zarchi*
ORGANIZATION LIAISON

*Mushky Lipskier*
PROGRAM COORDINATOR

*Mushka Majesky*
SCHOOL LIAISON

*Chumy Heber*
MARKETING

*Raizy Lifshitz*
COMMUNICATIONS

*Matti Feigelstock*
PROJECT L'CHAIM VANCOUVER

*Dovid Goldstein*
THE WELLNESS INSTITUTE—HOUSTON

### CLINICAL ADVISORY BOARD

*Tami D. Benton M.D., MHS*
*Thomas Joiner, PhD*
*E. David Klonsky, PhD*
*Madelyn Gould, PhD, MPH*
*Jill Harkavy-Friedman, PhD*
*Lisa Miller, PhD*
*Lisa A. Horowitz, PhD, MPH*
*David A. Brent, M.D.*
*Michele Borba, Ed.D.*
*Kenneth Ginsburg, M.D., M.S. Ed*
*Randal M. Ernst, Ed.D*
*Andrew Shatte, PHD*
*Laura H. Mufson, PhD*
*Jonathan Singer, PhD, LCSW*
*Arielle H. Sheftall, PhD*
*Tayyab Rashid, PhD*
*Casey Skvorc, PhD, JD*
*Sigrid Pechenik, PsyD*

### JLI INTERNATIONAL

*Rabbi Avrohom Sternberg*
CHAIRMAN

*Rabbi Dubi Rabinowitz*
DIRECTOR

*Rabbi Eli Wolf*
ADMINISTRATOR, JLI IN THE CIS
*In Partnership with the Federation of Jewish Communities of the CIS*

*Flor Setton*
COORDINATOR,
CHABAD OF ARGENTINA

*Rabbi Nochum Schapiro*
REGIONAL REPRESENTATIVE, AUSTRALIA

*Rabbi Avrohom Steinmetz*
REGIONAL REPRESENTATIVE, BRAZIL

*Rabbi Shevach Zlatopolsky*
EDITOR, JLI IN THE CIS

*Rabbi Shlomo Cohen*
FRENCH COORDINATOR,
REGIONAL REPRESENTATIVE

*Rabbi Avraham Golovacheov*
REGIONAL REPRESENTATIVE, GERMANY

*Rabbi Shlomo Koves*
REGIONAL REPRESENTATIVE, HUNGARY

*Rabbi Shmuel Katzman*
REGIONAL REPRESENTATIVE, NETHERLANDS

*Rabbi Bentzi Sudak*
REGIONAL REPRESENTATIVE,
UNITED KINGDOM

### NATIONAL JEWISH RETREAT

*Rabbi Hesh Epstein*
CHAIRMAN

*Mrs. Shaina B. Mintz*
DIRECTOR

*Bruce Backman*
HOTEL LIAISON

*Rabbi Shabsy Katz*
PROGRAM COORDINATOR

*Rabbi Isaac Mintz*
SHLUCHIM LIAISON

*Rabbi Mendel Rosenfeld*
LOGISTICS COORDINATOR

*Mrs. Aliza Scheinfeld*
*Ms. Mushka Silberstein*
SERVICE AND SUPPORT

### THE LAND & THE SPIRIT
**Israel Experience**

*Rabbi Isaac Mintz*
DIRECTOR

*Mrs. Shaina B. Mintz*
ADMINISTRATOR

*Rabbi Levi Moscowitz*
PROJECT MANAGER

*Ms. Esty Donin*
PARTICIPANT LIAISON

*Rabbi Yechiel Baitelman*
*Rabbi Dovid Flinkenstein*
*Rabbi Chanoch Kaplan*
*Rabbi Levi Klein*
*Rabbi Mendy Mangel*
*Rabbi Sholom Raichik*
STEERING COMMITTEE

### SHABBAT IN THE HEIGHTS

*Rabbi Isaac Mintz*
DIRECTOR

*Rabbi Avremi Rapoport*
SHLUCHIM LIAISON

*Mrs. Shulamis Nadler*
SERVICE AND SUPPORT

*Rabbi Chaim Hanoka*
CHAIRMAN

*Rabbi Mordechai Dinerman*
*Rabbi Zalman Marcus*
STEERING COMMITTEE

### MYSHIUR
**Advanced Learning Initiative**

*Rabbi Shmuel Kaplan*
CHAIRMAN

*Rabbi Shlomie Tenenbaum*
ADMINISTRATOR

### TORAHCAFE.COM
**Online Learning**

*Rabbi Mendy Elishevitz*
WEBSITE DEVELOPMENT

*Moshe Levin*
CONTENT MANAGER

*Mendel Laine*
FILMING

### OMEK INSTITUTE

*Rabbi Naftali Silberberg*
CURRICULUM DIRECTOR

*Ms. Sara Weiss*
DIRECTOR

*Mrs. Chana Marasow*
ADMINISTRATOR

*Rabbi Dr. Seth Grauer*
*Rabbi Moshe Weinberger*
*Rabbi Efrem Goldberg*
*Rabbi Menachem Penner*
ADVISORY BOARD

*Rabbi Zalman Leib Markowitz*
EDUCATIONAL CONSULTANT

### ALIBA DENAFSHEI

*Rabbi Mordechai Dinerman*
CURRICULUM DIRECTOR

*Rabbi Tzaly Dubov*
DIRECTOR

*Rabbi Shmuli Block*
EDITOR

### MACHON SHMUEL
**The Sami Rohr Research Institute**

*Rabbi Zalman Korf*
ADMINISTRATOR

*Rabbi Moshe Miller, OBM*
*Rabbi Gedalya Oberlander*
*Rabbi Chaim Rapoport*
*Rabbi Levi Yitzchak Raskin*
*Rabbi Chaim Schapiro*
RABBINIC ADVISORY BOARD

*Rabbi Yakov Gershon*
RESEARCH FELLOW

### FOUNDING DEPARTMENT HEADS

*Rabbi Mendel Bell*
*Rabbi Zalman Charytan*
*Rabbi Mendel Druk*
*Rabbi Menachem Gansburg*
*Rabbi Meir Hecht*
*Rabbi Levi Kaplan*
*Rabbi Yoni Katz*
*Rabbi Chaim Zalman Levy*
*Rabbi Benny Rapoport*
*Dr. Chana Silberstein*
*Rabbi Elchonon Tenenbaum*
*Rabbi Mendy Weg*

# JLI Chapter Directory

## ALABAMA

### BIRMINGHAM
*Rabbi Yossi Friedman* 205.970.0100

### MOBILE
*Rabbi Yosef Goldwasser* 251.265.1213

## ALASKA

### ANCHORAGE
*Rabbi Yosef Greenberg*
*Rabbi Mendy Greenberg* 907.357.8770

## ARIZONA

### CHANDLER
*Rabbi Mendy Deitsch* 480.855.4333

### FLAGSTAFF
*Rabbi Dovie Shapiro* 928.255.5756

### FOUNTAIN HILLS
*Rabbi Mendy Lipskier* 480.776.4763

### GLENDALE
*Rabbi Sholom Lew* 623.252.1759

### LAKE HAVASU CITY
*Rabbi Mendel Super* 928.706.6602

### ORO VALLEY
*Rabbi Ephraim Zimmerman* 520.477.8672

### PARADISE VALLEY
*Rabbi Shlomo Levertov* 480.788.9310

### PHOENIX
*Rabbi Dovber Dechter* 347.410.0785
*Rabbi Mendy Levertov* 602.861.1600
*Rabbi Yossi Friedman* 602.944.2753

### PRESCOTT
*Rabbi Elie Filler* 928.362.8924

### SCOTTSDALE
*Rabbi Yossi Levertov* 480.998.1410
*Rabbi Mendel Vaisfiche* 929.309.7811

### SEDONA
*Rabbi Mendel Kessler* 928.985.0667

### TUCSON
*Rabbi Yehuda Ceitlin* 520.881.7956

### VAIL
*Rabbi Yisroel Shemtov* 347.372.3092

## ARKANSAS

### LITTLE ROCK
*Rabbi Pinchus Ciment* 501.217.0053

## CALIFORNIA

### AGOURA HILLS
*Rabbi Moshe Bryski* 818.516.0444

### ALAMEDA
*Rabbi Meir Shmotkin* 510.640.2590

### ARCADIA
*Rabbi Sholom Stiefel* 626.539.4578

### BAKERSFIELD
*Rabbi Shmuli Schlanger* 661.834.1512

### BEL AIR
*Rabbi Chaim Mentz* 310.475.5311

### BEL AIR WEST
*Rabbi Mendy Mentz* 310.666.2302

### BEVERLY HILLS
*Rabbi Dovid Begun* 310.242.7750

### BEVERLYWOOD
*Rabbi Menachem Mendel Piekarski* 310.597.0967

### BURBANK
*Rabbi Shmuly Kornfeld* 818.954.0070

### CARLSBAD
*Rabbi Yeruchem Eilfort*
*Mrs. Nechama Eilfort* 760.943.8891

### CERRITOS
*Rabbi Mendel Lehrer* 917.717.8704

### CHATSWORTH
*Rabbi Yossi Spritzer* 818.307.9907

### CHULA VISTA
*Rabbi Mendel Katz* 347.554.1801

### CONCORD
*Rabbi Berel Kesselman* 925.326.1613

### CONTRA COSTA
*Rabbi Dovber Berkowitz* 925.937.4101

### CORONADO
*Rabbi Eli Fradkin* 619.365.4728

### DANA POINT
*Rabbi Eli Goorevitch* 949.290.0628

### DANVILLE
*Rabbi Shmuli Raitman* 213.447.6694

### EMERYVILLE
*Rabbi Menachem Blank* 510.859.8808

### ENCINO
*Rabbi Aryeh Herzog* 818.784.9986
*Chapter founded by Rabbi Joshua Gordon, OBM*

### FOLSOM
*Rabbi Yossi Grossbaum* 916.608.9811

### FREMONT
*Rabbi Eli Landes* 510.300.4090

### GLENDALE
*Rabbi Simcha Backman* 818.240.2750

### HIGHLAND PARK
*Rabbi Mendel Korf* 323.872.4876

### HOLLYWOOD
*Rabbi Zalman Partouche* 818.964.9428

### HUNTINGTON BEACH
*Rabbi Aron David Berkowitz* 714.846.2285

### IRVINE
*Rabbi Elly Andrusier* 949.786.5000

### LAGUNA NIGUEL
*Rabbi Mendy Paltiel* 949.201.92311

**LA JOLLA**

*Rabbi Baruch Shalom Ezagui* 858.455.5433

**LAKE BALBOA**

*Rabbi Eli Gurary* 347.403.6734

**LOMITA**

*Rabbi Sholom Pinson* 310.326.8234

**LONG BEACH**

*Rabbi Abba Perelmuter* 562.773.1350

**LOS ANGELES**

*Rabbi Yigal Begun* 347.933.8174
*Rabbi Yossi Elifort* 310.515.5310
*Rabbi Leibel Korf* 323.660.5177
*Rabbi Zalmy Labkowsky* 213.618.9486
*Rabbi Mendel Zajac* 310.770.9051

**MALIBU**

*Rabbi Levi Cunin* 310.456.6588

**MAR VISTA**

*Rabbi Shimon Simpson* 646.401.2354

**MARINA DEL REY**

*Rabbi Danny Yiftach-Hashem*
*Rabbi Dovid Yiftach* 310.859.0770

**MILL VALLEY**

*Rabbi Hillel Scop* 415.336.3055

**MISSION VIEJO**

*Rabbi Zalman Marcus* 949.689.5159

**NEWHALL**

*Rabbi Choni Marosov* 661.254.3434

**NEWPORT BEACH**

*Rabbi Reuven Mintz* 949.375.3707

**NORTHRIDGE**

*Rabbi Eli Rivkin* 818.368.3937

**OJAI**

*Rabbi Mordechai Nemtzov* 805.613.7181

**OXNARD**

*Rabbi Dov Muchnik* 805.844.9989

**PACIFIC PALISADES**

*Rabbi Avi Cunin* 310.454.7783

**PALO ALTO**

*Rabbi Yosef Levin* 650.804.8910
*Rabbi Zalman Levin* 650.424.9800

**PASADENA**

*Rabbi Zushe Rivkin* 626.788.3343

**PLEASANTON**

*Rabbi Josh Zebberman* 925.846.0700

**PORTOLA VALLEY**

*Rabbi Mayer Brook* 650.304.2098

**POWAY**

*Rabbi Mendel Goldstein* 858.208.6613

**RANCHO CUCAMONGA**

*Rabbi Sholom Ber Harlig* 909.949.4553

**RANCHO MIRAGE**

*Rabbi Shimon H. Posner* 760.770.7785

**RANCHO PALOS VERDES**

*Rabbi Yitzchok Magalnic* 310.544.5544

**RANCHO S. FE**

*Rabbi Levi Raskin* 858.756.7571

**REDONDO BEACH**

*Rabbi Yossi Mintz*
*Rabbi Zalman Gordon* 310.214.4999

**RESEDA**

*Rabbi Hershy Spritzer* 818.881.1033

**RIVERSIDE**

*Rabbi Shmuel Fuss* 951.329.2747

**S. ANSELMO**

*Rabbi Moshe Berkowitz* 415.910.8186

**S. CLEMENTE**

*Rabbi Menachem M. Slavin* 949.489.0723

**S. CRUZ**

*Rabbi Yochanan Friedman* 831.454.0101

**S. DIEGO**

*Rabbi Rafi Andrusier* 619.387.8770
*Rabbi Yechiel Cagen* 832.216.1534
*Rabbi Motte Fradkin* 858.547.0076

**S. FRANCISCO**

*Rabbi Yakov Barber* 424.499.9868
*Rebbetzin Mattie Pil* 415.933.4310
*Rabbi Gedalia Potash* 415.648.8000
*Rabbi Shlomo Zarchi* 415.752.2866

**S. LUIS OBISPO**

*Rabbi Meir Gordon* 347.675.3383

**S. MATEO**

*Rabbi Yossi Marcus* 650.341.4510

**S. RAFAEL**

*Rabbi Yisrael Rice* 415.492.1666

**SHERMAN OAKS**

*Rabbi Nachman Abend* 818.989.9539

**SONOMA**

*Rabbi Mendel Wolvovsky* 707.292.6221

**SOUTH LAKE TAHOE**

*Rabbi Mordechai Richler* 530.539.4363

**SOUTH PASADENA**

*Rabbi Dovid Harlig* 626.921.6256

**STOCKHOLM**

*Rabbi Avremel Brod* 209.952.2081

**SUNNYVALE**

*Rabbi Yisroel Hecht* 408.720.0553

**TEMECULA**

*Rabbi Yonason Abrams* 951.234.4196

**TIBURON**

*Rabbi Levi Mintz* 415.378.9364

**TOPANGA**

*Rabbi Menachem Piekarski* 858.335.7197

**TUSTIN**

*Rabbi Yehoshua Eliezrie* 714.508.2150

**VACAVILLE**

*Rabbi Chaim Zaklos* 707.592.5300

**WEST HILLS**

*Rabbi Avi Rabin* 818.337.4544

#### WEST HOLLYWOOD
*Rabbi Mordechai Kirschenbaum* 310.691.9988

#### WEST LOS ANGELES
*Rabbi Mordechai Zaetz* 424.652.8742

#### WOODLAND HILLS
*Rabbi Menachem Mendel Gordon* 818.917.8456

#### YORBA LINDA
*Rabbi Dovid Eliezrie* 714.693.0770

### COLORADO

#### ASPEN
*Rabbi Mendel Mintz* 970.544.3770

#### BROOMFIELD
*Rabbi Yossi Rapoport* 720.968.0086

#### DENVER
*Rabbi Mendel Popack* 720.515.4337
*Rabbi Yossi Serebryanski* 303.744.9699
*Rabbi Mendy Sirota* 720.940.3716

#### FORT COLLINS
*Rabbi Yerachmiel Gorelik* 970.407.1613

#### HIGHLANDS RANCH
*Rabbi Avraham Mintz* 303.694.9119

#### LONGMONT
*Rabbi Yakov Borenstein* 303.678.7595

#### VAIL
*Rabbi Dovid Mintz* 970.476.7887

#### WESTMINSTER
*Rabbi Benjy Brackman* 303.429.5177

### CONNECTICUT

#### FAIRFIELD
*Rabbi Shlame Landa* 203.373.7551

#### GLASTONBURY
*Rabbi Yosef Wolvovsky* 860.659.2422

#### GREENWICH
*Rabbi Yossi Deren*
*Rabbi Menachem Feldman* 203.629.9059

#### GUILFORD
*Rabbi Yossi Yaffe* 203.645.4635

#### HAMDEN
*Rabbi Moshe Hecht* 203.635.7268

#### LITCHFIELD
*Rabbi Joseph Eisenbach* 860.567.3377

#### MILFORD
*Rabbi Schneur Wilhelm* 203.887.7603

#### NEW HAVEN
*Rabbi Mendy Hecht* 203.589.5375
*Rabbi Chanoch Wineberg* 203.479.0313

#### NEW LONDON
*Rabbi Avrohom Sternberg* 860.437.8000

#### ORANGE
*Rabbi Hershy Hecht* 203.464.7809

#### OXFORD
*Rabbi Shmaya Hecht* 203.514.0622

#### SHELTON
*Rabbi Schneur Brook* 203.364.4149

#### STAMFORD
*Rabbi Yisrael Deren*
*Rabbi Levi Mendelow* 203.3.CHABAD

#### WEST HARTFORD
*Rabbi Shaya Gopin* 860.232.1116

#### WESTPORT
*Rabbi Yehuda Kantor* 561.460.3758

### DELAWARE

#### WILMINGTON
*Rabbi Chuni Vogel* 302.529.9900

### DISTRICT OF COLUMBIA
*Rabbi Levi Shemtov*
*Rabbi Yitzy Ceitlin* 202.332.5600

### FLORIDA

#### ALTAMONTE SPRINGS
*Rabbi Mendy Bronstein* 407.280.0535

#### AVENTURA
*Rabbi Yossi Itkin* 347.300.0439
*Rabbi Mendel Rosenblum* 412.807.0584

#### BOCA RATON
*Rabbi Zalman Bukiet* 561.487.2934
*Rabbi Moishe Denburg* 561.526.5760
*Rabbi Arele Gopin* 561.994.6257
*Rabbi Ruvi New* 561.394.9770

#### BONITA SPRINGS
*Rabbi Mendy Greenberg* 239.949.6900

#### BOYNTON BEACH
*Rabbi Sholom Ciment* 561.732.4633
*Rabbi Yosef Yitzchok Raichik* 561.740.8738

#### BRADENTON
*Rabbi Menachem Bukiet* 941.388.9656

#### CAPE CORAL
*Rabbi Yossi Labkowski* 239.963.4770

#### CLERMONT
*Rabbi Moshe Dubinsky* 862.812.2174

#### CORAL GABLES
*Rabbi Avraham Stolik* 305.490.7572

#### CORAL SPRINGS
*Rabbi Hershy Bronstein* 954.798.6023
*Rabbi Yankie Denburg* 954.471.8646

#### CUTLER BAY
*Rabbi Yossi Wolff* 305.975.6680

#### DAVIE
*Rabbi Aryeh Schwartz* 954.376.9973

#### DELRAY BEACH
*Rabbi Yaakov Perman* 561.666.2770

#### FISHER ISLAND
*Rabbi Efraim Brody* 347.325.1913

#### FLEMING ISLAND
*Rabbi Shmuly Feldman* 904.290.1017

#### FORT LAUDERDALE
*Rabbi Schneur Kaplan* 954.667.8000
*Rabbi Yitzchok Naparstek* 954.568.1190

#### FORT MYERS
*Rabbi Yitzchok Minkowicz* 239.433.7708

**HALLANDALE BEACH**

*Rabbi Mordy Feiner* 954.458.1877

**HOLLYWOOD**

*Rabbi Leizer Barash* 954.549.5012
*Rabbi Leibel Kudan* 954.801.3367

**JUPITER**

*Rabbi Berel Barash* 561.317.0968

**KENDALL**

*Rabbi Yossi Harlig* 305.234.5654

**KEY BISCAYNE**

*Rabbi Avremel Caroline* 305.365.6744

**LAKE WORTH**

*Rabbi Zalmen Itkin* 917.445.1973

**LAUDERHILL**

*Rabbi Shmuel Heidingsfeld* 323.877.7703

**LONGWOOD**

*Rabbi Yanky Majesky* 407.636.5994

**MAITLAND**

*Rabbi Sholom Dubov*
*Rabbi Levik Dubov* 470.644.2500

**MARION COUNTY**

*Rabbi Yossi Hecht* 352.330.4466

**MIAMI**

*Rabbi Mendy Cheruty* 305.219.3353
*Rabbi Yakov Fellig* 305.445.5444
*Rabbi Shmuel Gopin* 305.573.9995
*Rabbi Chaim Lipskar* 305.373.8303

**MIAMI BEACH**

*Rabbi Yisroel Frankforter* 305.534.3895
*Rabbi Sholom Korf* 786.423.6483
*Rabbi Shmuel Mann* 305.674.8400

**NAPLES**

*Rabbi Fishel Zaklos* 239.404.6993

**N. MIAMI BEACH**

*Rabbi Leib Ezagui* 561.596.0530
*Rabbi Yehoshua Karp* 862.226.2869
*Rabbi Eli Laufer* 305.770.4412

**ORLANDO**

*Rabbi Yosef Konikov* 407.354.3660

**ORMOND BEACH**

*Rabbi Asher Farkash* 386.672.9300

**OVEIDO**

*Rabbi Tzviky Dubov* 407.529.8256

**PALM BEACH**

*Rabbi Zalman Levitin* 561.659.3884

**PALM BEACH GARDENS**

*Rabbi Dovid Vigler* 561.624.2223

**PALM CITY**

*Rabbi Shlomo Uminer* 772.485.5501

**PALM HARBOR**

*Rabbi Pinchas Adler* 727.789.0408

**PARKLAND**

*Rabbi Mendy Gutnick* 954.600.6991

**PEMBROKE PINES**

*Rabbi Mordechai Andrusier* 954.874.2280

**PENSACOLA**

*Rabbi Mendel Danow* 850.291.9600

**PLANTATION**

*Rabbi Pinchas Taylor* 954.644.9177

**PONTE VEDRA BEACH**

*Rabbi Nochum Kurinsky* 904.543.9301

**PORT ORANGE**

*Rabbi Mendel Niasoff* 386.679.5756

**ROYAL PALM BEACH**

*Rabbi Nachmen Zeev Schtroks* 561.714.1692

**S. AUGUSTINE**

*Rabbi Levi Vogel* 904.521.8664

**S. JOHNS**

*Rabbi Mendel Sharfstein* 347.461.3765

**S. PETERSBURG**

*Rabbi Alter Korf* 727.344.4900

**SARASOTA**

*Rabbi Chaim Shaul Steinmetz* 941.925.0770
*Rabbi Levi Steinmetz* 941.928.9267

**SATELLITE BEACH**

*Rabbi Zvi Konikov* 321.777.2770

**SINGER ISLAND**

*Rabbi Berel Namdar* 347.276.6985

**SOUTH PALM BEACH**

*Rabbi Leibel Stolik* 561.889.3499

**SOUTH TAMPA**

*Rabbi Mendy Dubrowski* 813.922.1723

**SOUTHWEST BROWARD COUNTY**

*Rabbi Aryeh Schwartz* 954.252.1770

**SUNNY ISLES BEACH**

*Rabbi Alexander Kaller* 305.803.5315

**SURFSIDE**

*Rabbi Dov Schochet* 305.790.8294

**TAMARAC**

*Rabbi Kopel Silberberg* 954.882.7434

**TAMPA**

*Rabbi Chaim Lipszyc* 954.882.7434

**VENICE**

*Rabbi Sholom Ber Schmerling* 845.238.0770

**VERO BEACH**

*Rabbi Motty Rosenfeld* 772.245.6712

**WATERWAYS**

*Rabbi Yisroel Brusowankin* 786.663.8731

**WESLEY CHAPEL**

*Rabbi Mendy Yarmush*
*Rabbi Mendel Friedman* 813.731.2977

**WEST DELRAY BEACH**

*Rabbi Yossi Schapiro* 561.221.1618

**WEST PALM BEACH**

*Rabbi Yoel Gancz* 561.659.7770

**WESTON**

*Rabbi Yisroel Spalter* 954.349.6565

## GEORGIA

**ALPHARETTA**

*Rabbi Hirshy Minkowicz* 770.410.9000

### ATLANTA

*Rabbi Yossi New*
*Rabbi Isser New* 404.843.2464
*Rabbi Alexander Piekarski* 678.267.6418
*Rabbi Ari Sollish* 404.898.0434

### ATLANTA: INTOWN

*Rabbi Eliyahu Schusterman*
*Rabbi Chanan Rose* 415.370.1333

### AUGUSTA

*Rabbi Zalman Fischer* 706.836.1576

### CUMMING

*Rabbi Levi Mentz* 310.666.2218

### DUNWOODY

*Rabbi Mendy Wineberg* 347.770.2414

### GAINESVILLE

*Rabbi Nechemia Gurevitz* 770.906.4970

### GWINNETT

*Rabbi Yossi Lerman* 678.595.0196

### MARIETTA

*Rabbi Ephraim Silverman* 770.565.4412

### ROSWELL

*Rabbi Chaim Schwartz* 770.363.4644

## HAWAII

### KAILUA-KONA

*Rabbi Levi Gerlitzky* 917.853.2787

### KAPA'A

*Rabbi Michoel Goldman* 808.647.4293

## IDAHO

### BOISE

*Rabbi Mendel Lifshitz* 208.853.9200

## ILLINOIS

### ARLINGTON HEIGHTS

*Rabbi Yaakov Kotlarsky* 224.357.7002

### CHAMPAIGN

*Rabbi Dovid Tiechtel* 217.355.8672

### CHICAGO

*Rabbi Mendy Benhiyoun* 312.498.7704
*Rabbi Mordechai Gershon* 773.412.5189
*Rabbi Dovid Kotlarsky* 773.495.7127
*Rabbi Yosef Moscowitz* 773.772.3770
*Rabbi Levi Notik* 773.274.5123

### ELGIN

*Rabbi Mendel Shemtov* 847.440.4486

### GLENVIEW

*Rabbi Yishaya Benjaminson* 847.910.1738

### GURNEE

*Rabbi Sholom Tenenbaum* 847.782.1800

### HIGHLAND PARK

*Mrs. Michla Schanowitz* 847.266.0770

### NAPERVILLE

*Rabbi Mendy Goldstein* 630.957.8122

### NORTHBROOK

*Rabbi Meir Moscowitz* 847.564.8770

### NORWOOD PARK

*Rabbi Mendel Perlstein* 312.752.8894

### OAK PARK

*Rabbi Yitzchok Bergstein* 708.524.1530

### PARK RIDGE

*Rabbi Lazer Hershkovich* 224.392.4442

### PEORIA

*Rabbi Eli Langsam* 309.370.7701

### RIVERWOODS

*Rabbi Sholom Notik* 847.208.8794

### SKOKIE

*Rabbi Yochanan Posner* 847.677.1770

### VERNON HILLS

*Rabbi Shimmy Susskind* 718.755.5356

### WILMETTE

*Rabbi Dovid Flinkenstein* 847.251.7707

## INDIANA

### INDIANAPOLIS

*Rabbi Avraham Grossbaum*
*Rabbi Dr. Shmuel Klatzkin* 317.251.5573

## IOWA

### BETTENDORF

*Rabbi Shneur Cadaner* 563.355.1065

## KANSAS

### OVERLAND PARK

*Rabbi Mendy Wineberg* 913.649.4852

## KENTUCKY

### LOUISVILLE

*Rabbi Avrohom Litvin* 502.459.1770

## LOUISIANA

### BATON ROUGE

*Rabbi Peretz Kazen* 225.267.7047

### METAIRIE

*Rabbi Yossie Nemes*
*Rabbi Mendel Ceitlin* 504.454.2910

### NEW ORLEANS

*Rabbi Mendel Rivkin* 504.302.1830

## MAINE

### BANGOR

*Rabbi Chaim Wilansky* 207.650.7223

### PORTLAND

*Rabbi Levi Wilansky* 207.650.1783

## MARYLAND

### BALTIMORE

*Rabbi Velvel Belinsky* 410.764.5000
Classes in Russian

*Rabbi Dovid Reyder* 781.796.4204

### BEL AIR

*Rabbi Kushi Schusterman* 443.353.9718

### BETHESDA

*Rabbi Sender Geisinsky* 301.913.9777

### CHEVY CHASE

*Rabbi Zalman Minkowitz* 301.260.5000

**COLUMBIA**

*Rabbi Hillel Baron*
*Rabbi Yosef Chaim Sufrin* 410.740.2424

**FREDERICK**

*Rabbi Boruch Labkowski* 301.996.3659

**GAITHERSBURG**

*Rabbi Sholom Raichik* 301.926.3632

**OLNEY**

*Rabbi Bentzy Stolik* 301.660.6770

**OWINGS MILLS**

*Rabbi Nochum Katsenelenbogen* 410.356.5156

**POTOMAC**

*Rabbi Mendel Bluming* 301.983.4200
*Rabbi Mendel Kaplan* 301.983.1485

**ROCKVILLE**

*Rabbi Shlomo Beitsh* 646.773.2675
*Rabbi Moishe Kavka* 301.836.1242

## MASSACHUSETTS

**ANDOVER**

*Rabbi Asher Bronstein* 978.470.2288

**ARLINGTON**

*Rabbi Avi Bukiet* 617.909.8653

**BOSTON**

*Rabbi Yosef Zaklos* 617.297.7282

**BRIGHTON**

*Rabbi Dan Rodkin* 617.787.2200

**CAPE COD**

*Rabbi Yekusiel Alperowitz* 508.775.2324

**CHESTNUT HILL**

*Rabbi Mendy Uminer* 617.738.9770

**LEXINGTON**

*Rabbi Yisroel New* 646.248.9053

**LONGMEADOW**

*Rabbi Yakov Wolff* 413.567.8665

**NEWTON**

*Rabbi Shalom Ber Prus* 617.244.1200

**PEABODY**

*Rabbi Nechemia Schusterman* 978.977.9111

**SHARON**

*Rabbi Naftoli Minkowitz* 781.363.7066

**SOUTH SHORE**

*Rabbi Levi Lezell* 617.862.2770

**SUDBURY**

*Rabbi Yisroel Freeman* 978.443.0110

**SWAMPSCOTT**

*Rabbi Yossi Lipsker* 781.581.3833

**VINEYARD HAVEN**

*Rabbi Tzvi Alperowitz* 508.560.8650

## MICHIGAN

**ANN ARBOR**

*Rabbi Aharon Goldstein* 734.995.3276

**BLOOMFIELD HILLS**

*Rabbi Levi Dubov* 248.949.6210

**GRAND RAPIDS**

*Rabbi Mordechai Haller* 616.957.0770

**TROY**

*Rabbi Menachem Caytak* 248.873.5851

**WEST BLOOMFIELD**

*Rabbi Zelig Shemtov* 248.788.4000
*Rabbi Elimelech Silberberg* 248.855.6170

## MINNESOTA

**MINNETONKA**

*Rabbi Mordechai Grossbaum*
*Rabbi Shmuel Silberstein* 952.929.9922

**PLYMOUTH**

*Rabbi Nissan Naparstek* 310.430.0960

**S. PAUL**

*Rabbi Shneur Zalman Bendet* 651.998.9298

## MISSOURI

**CHESTERFIELD**

*Rabbi Avi Rubenfeld* 314.258.3401

**S. LOUIS**

*Rabbi Yosef Abenson* 314.448.0927
*Rabbi Yosef Landa* 314.725.0400

## MONTANA

**BOZEMAN**

*Rabbi Chaim Shaul Bruk* 406.600.4934

**KALISPELL**

*Rabbi Shneur Wolf* 406.885.2541

## NEVADA

**LAS VEGAS**

*Rabbi Yosef Rivkin* 702.217.2170

**RENO**

*Rabbi Levi Sputz* 347.262.4531

**SUMMERLIN**

*Rabbi Yisroel Schanowitz*
*Rabbi Tzvi Bronchtain* 702.855.0770

## NEW JERSEY

**BASKING RIDGE**

*Rabbi Mendy Herson*
*Rabbi Mendel Shemtov* 908.604.8844

**CHERRY HILL**

*Rabbi Mendel Mangel* 856.874.1500

**CLINTON**

*Rabbi Eli Kornfeld* 908.623.7000

**ENGLEWOOD**

*Rabbi Shmuel Konikov* 201.519.7343

**FAIR LAWN**

*Rabbi Avrohom Bergstein* 201.794.3770

**FANWOOD**

*Rabbi Avrohom Blesofsky* 908.790.0008

**FLANDERS**

*Rabbi Yaacov Shusterman* 973.723.6868

**FORT LEE**

*Rabbi Meir Konikov* 201.886.1238

**GREATER MERCER COUNTY**

*Rabbi Dovid Dubov*
*Rabbi Yaakov Chaiton* 609.213.4136

**HASKELL**

*Rabbi Mendy Gurkov* 201.696.7609

**HOLMDEL**

*Rabbi Shmaya Galperin* 732.772.1998

**JACKSON**

*Rabbi Shmuel Naparstek* 732.668.7702

**MADISON**

*Rabbi Shalom Lubin* 973.377.0707

**MANALAPAN**

*Rabbi Boruch Chazanow* 732.972.3687
Chapter founded by Rabbi Levi Wolosow, OBM

**MEDFORD**

*Rabbi Yitzchok Kahan* 609.451.3522

**MENDHAM**

*Rabbi Ari Herson* 732.619.8829

**MONTCLAIR**

*Rabbi Yaacov Leaf* 862.252.5666

**MORRISTOWN**

*Rabbi Moishe Gurevitz* 973.216.8077

**MOUNTAIN LAKES**

*Rabbi Levi Dubinsky* 973.551.1898

**MULLICA HILL**

*Rabbi Avrohom Richler* 856.733.0770

**OLD TAPPAN**

*Rabbi Mendy Lewis* 201.767.4008

**RANDOLPH**

*Rabbi Avraham Bekhor* 973.723.0933

**RED BANK**

*Rabbi Dovid Harrison* 973.895.3070

**ROCKAWAY**

*Rabbi Asher Herson*
*Rabbi Mordechai Baumgarten* 973.625.1525

**RUTHERFORD**

*Rabbi Yitzchok Lerman* 347.834.7500

**SCOTCH PLAINS**

*Rabbi Avrohom Blesofsky* 908.790.0008

**SHORT HILLS**

*Rabbi Mendel Solomon*
*Rabbi Avrohom Levin* 973.725.7008

**SOUTH BRUNSWICK**

*Rabbi Levi Azimov* 732.398.9492

**TENAFLY**

*Rabbi Mordechai Shain* 201.871.1152

**TOMS RIVER**

*Rabbi Moshe Gourarie* 732.349.4199

**VENTNOR**

*Rabbi Avrohom Rapoport* 609.822.8500

**WEST ORANGE**

*Rabbi Mendy Kasowitz* 973.325.6311

**WOODCLIFF LAKE**

*Rabbi Dov Drizin* 201.476.0157

## NEW MEXICO

**ALBUQUERQUE**

*Rabbi Chaim Schmukler* 505.236.8470

**LAS CRUCES**

*Rabbi Bery Schmukler* 575.524.1330

**S. FE**

*Rabbi Berel Levertov* 505.920.4324

## NEW YORK

**ALBANY**

*Rabbi Mordechai Rubin* 518.368.7886

**BEDFORD**

*Rabbi Arik Wolf* 914.666.6065

**BENSONHURST**

*Rabbi Avrohom Hertz* 718.753.7768

**BINGHAMTON**

*Mrs. Rivkah Slonim* 607.797.0015

**BRIGHTON BEACH**

*Rabbi Dovid Okonov* 718.368.4490

**BRONXVILLE**

*Rabbi Sruli Deitsch* 917.755.0078

**BROOKVILLE**

*Rabbi Mendy Heber* 516.626.0600

**CEDARHURST**

*Rabbi Zalman Wolowik* 516.295.2478

**CLIFTON PARK**

*Rabbi Yossi Rubin* 518.495.0772

**COMMACK**

*Rabbi Mendel Teldon* 631.543.3343

**DELMAR**

*Rabbi Zalman Simon* 518.866.7658

**DOBBS FERRY**

*Rabbi Benjy Silverman* 914.693.6100

**EAST HAMPTON**

*Rabbi Leibel Baumgarten*
*Rabbi Mendy Goldberg* 631.329.5800

**ELLENVILLE**

*Rabbi Shlomie Deren* 845.647.4450

**FOREST HILLS**

*Rabbi Yossi Mendelson* 917.861.9726

**GLEN OAKS**

*Rabbi Shmuel Nadler* 347.388.7064

**GREAT NECK**

*Rabbi Yoseph Geisinsky* 516.487.4554

**HOWARD BEACH**

*Rabbi Avrohom Richler* 917.541.7374

**ISLIP**

*Rabbi Shimon Stillerman* 631.913.8770

**KINGSTON**

*Rabbi Yitzchok Hecht* 845.334.9044

**LARCHMONT**

*Rabbi Mendel Silberstein* 914.834.4321

**LITTLE NECK**

*Rabbi Eli Shifrin* 718.423.1235

**LONG BEACH**

*Rabbi Eli Goodman* 516.574.3905

LONG ISLAND CITY

*Rabbi Zev Wineberg* 347.218.2927

MANHASSET

*Rabbi Mendel Paltiel* 516.984.0701

MELVILLE

*Rabbi Yosef Raskin* 631.276.4453

MINEOLA

*Rabbi Anchelle Perl* 516.739.3636

NEW HARTFORD

*Rabbi Levi Charitonow* 716.322.8692

NEW YORK

*Rabbi Yakov Bankhalter* 917.613.1678
*Rabbi Nissi Eber* 347.677.2276
*Rabbi Berel Gurevitch* 212.518.3122
*Rabbi Daniel Kraus* 917.294.5567
*Rabbi Shmuel Metzger* 212.758.3770

NYC TRIBECA

*Rabbi Zalman Paris* 212.566.6764

NYC UPPER EAST SIDE

*Rabbi Uriel Vigler* 212.369.7310

NYC WEST SIDE

*Rabbi Shlomo Kugel* 212.864.5010

OCEANSIDE

*Rabbi Levi Gurkow* 516.764.7385

OSSINING

*Rabbi Dovid Labkowski* 914.923.2522

OYSTER BAY

*Rabbi Shmuel Lipszyc*
*Rabbi Shalom Lipszyc* 347.853.9992

PARK SLOPE

*Rabbi Menashe Wolf* 347.957.1291

PORT WASHINGTON

*Rabbi Shalom Paltiel* 516.767.8672

PROSPECT HEIGHTS

*Rabbi Mendy Hecht* 347.622.3599

ROCHESTER

*Rabbi Nechemia Vogel* 585.271.0330

ROSLYN

*Rabbi Yaakov Reiter* 516.484.3500

ROSLYN HEIGHTS

*Rabbi Aaron Konikov* 516.484.3500

SEA GATE

*Rabbi Chaim Brikman* 347.524.3214

SOUTHAMPTON

*Rabbi Chaim Pape* 917.627.4865

STATEN ISLAND

*Rabbi Mendy Katzman* 718.370.8953

STONY BROOK

*Rabbi Shalom Ber Cohen* 631.585.0521

SUFFERN

*Rabbi Shmuel Gancz* 845.368.1889

WEST BRIGHTON BEACH

*Rabbi Moshe Winner* 718.946.9833

YORKTOWN HEIGHTS

*Rabbi Yehuda Heber* 914.962.1111

## NORTH CAROLINA

ASHEVILLE

*Rabbi Shaya Susskind* 828.335.4604

CARY

*Rabbi Yisroel Cotlar* 919.651.9710

CHAPEL HILL

*Rabbi Zalman Bluming* 919.357.5904

CHARLOTTE

*Rabbi Yossi Groner*
*Rabbi Shlomo Cohen* 704.366.3984

GREENSBORO

*Rabbi Yosef Plotkin* 336.617.8120

RALEIGH

*Rabbi Pinchas Herman*
*Rabbi Mendy Wilschanski* 919.847.8986

WILMINGTON

*Rabbi Moshe Lieblich* 910.763.4770

WINSTON-SALEM

*Rabbi Levi Gurevitz* 336.756.9069

## OHIO

BEACHWOOD

*Rabbi Moshe Gancz* 216.647.4884

CINCINNATI

*Rabbi Yisroel Mangel* 513.793.5200

COLUMBUS

*Rabbi Shea Kaltmann* 614.935.2804
*Rabbi Yitzi Kaltmann* 614.294.3296

DAYTON

*Rabbi Nochum Mangel* 937.643.0770

TWINSBURG

*Rabbi Mendy Greenberg* 440.465.2063

## OKLAHOMA

OKLAHOMA CITY

*Rabbi Ovadia Goldman* 405.524.4800

TULSA

*Rabbi Yehuda Weg* 918.492.4499

## OREGON

PORTLAND

*Rabbi Mordechai Wilhelm* 503.977.9947

SALEM

*Rabbi Avrohom Yitzchok Perlstein* 503.383.9569

TIGARD

*Rabbi Menachem Orenstein* 971.329.6661

WEST LINN

*Rabbi Shimon Wilhelm* 503.753.4744

## PENNSYLVANIA

AMBLER

*Rabbi Shaya Deitsch* 215.591.9310

BALA CYNWYD

*Rabbi Shraga Sherman* 610.660.9192

CLARKS SUMMIT

*Rabbi Benny Rapoport* 570.587.3300

### DOYLESTOWN

*Rabbi Mendel Prus* 215.340.1303

### FAIRMONT

*Rabbi Hirshi Sputz* 267.332.1321

### FREEDOM

*Rabbi Yosef Feller* 612.275.6438

### GLEN MILLS

*Rabbi Yehuda Gerber* 484.620.4162

### LAFAYETTE HILL

*Rabbi Yisroel Kotlarsky* 484.533.7009

### LANCASTER

*Rabbi Elazar Green* 717.723.8783

### LEWISBURG

*Rabbi Yisroel Baumgarten* 631.880.2801

### MECHANICSBURG

*Rabbi Nissen Pewzner* 717.798.0053

### MONROEVILLE

*Rabbi Mendy Schapiro* 412.372.1000

### NEWTOWN

*Rabbi Aryeh Weinstein* 215.497.9925

### PHILADELPHIA

*Rabbi Berel Paltiel* 718.288.8574

### PHILADELPHIA: CENTER CITY

*Rabbi Yochonon Goldman* 215.238.2100

### PITTSBURGH

*Rabbi Yisroel Altein* 412.422.7300 EXT. 269

### PITTSBURGH: SOUTH HILLS

*Rabbi Mendy Rosenblum* 412.278.3693

### READING

*Rabbi Yosef Lipsker* 610.334.3218

### RYDAL

*Rabbi Zushe Gurevitz* 267.536.5757

### UNIVERSITY PARK

*Rabbi Nosson Meretsky* 814.863.4929

### WYNNEWOOD

*Rabbi Moishe Brennan* 610.529.9011

## PUERTO RICO

### CAROLINA

*Rabbi Mendel Zarchi* 787.253.0894

## RHODE ISLAND

### WARWICK

*Rabbi Yossi Laufer* 401.884.7888

## SOUTH CAROLINA

### BLUFFTON

*Rabbi Menachem Hertz* 843.301.1819

### COLUMBIA

*Rabbi Hesh Epstein*
*Rabbi Levi Marrus* 803.782.1831

### GREENVILLE

*Rabbi Leibel Kesselman* 864.534.7739

### MYRTLE BEACH

*Rabbi Doron Aizenman* 843.448.0035

## TENNESSEE

### CHATTANOOGA

*Rabbi Shaul Perlstein* 423.910.9770

### KNOXVILLE

*Rabbi Yossi Wilhelm* 865.300.8012

### MEMPHIS

*Rabbi Levi Klein* 901.754.0404

### NASHVILLE

*Rabbi Yitzchok Tiechtel* 615.646.5750

## TEXAS

### AUSTIN

*Rabbi Mendy Levertov* 512.905.2778

### BELLAIRE

*Rabbi Yossi Zaklikofsky* 713.839.8887

### CYPRESS

*Rabbi Levi Marinovsky* 832.651.6964

### DALLAS

*Rabbi Zvi Drizin* 214.632.2633
*Rabbi Mendel Dubrawsky* 214.215.1540
*Rabbi Boruch Hecht* 310.704.5403
*Rabbi Moshe Naparstek* 972.818.0770

### EL PASO

*Rabbi Levi Greenberg* 347.678.9762

### FORT WORTH

*Rabbi Dov Mandel* 817.263.7701

### FRISCO

*Rabbi Mendy Kesselman* 214.460.7773

### HOUSTON

*Rabbi Dovid Goldstein*
*Rabbi Zally Lazarus* 281.589.7188
*Rabbi Moishe Traxler* 713.774.0300

### HOUSTON: RICE UNIVERSITY AREA

*Rabbi Eliezer Lazaroff* 713.522.2004

### LEAGUE CITY

*Rabbi Yitzchok Schmukler* 281.724.1554

### PLANO

*Rabbi Eli Block* 214.620.4083
*Rabbi Mendel Block* 972.596.8270

### ROCKWALL

*Rabbi Moshe Kalmenson* 469.350.5735

### ROUND ROCK

*Rabbi Mendel Marasow* 512.387.3171

### S. ANTONIO

*Rabbi Chaim Block*
*Rabbi Levi Teldon* 210.492.1085
*Rabbi Tal Shaul* 210.877.4218

### SOUTHLAKE

*Rabbi Levi Gurevitch* 817.451.1171

### SUGAR LAND

*Rabbi Ari Feigenson*
*Rabbi Mendel Feigenson* 832.758.0685

### THE WOODLANDS

*Rabbi Mendel Blecher* 281.865.7242

## UTAH

#### LEHI

*Rabbi Chaim Zippel* 801.674.4566

#### PARK CITY

*Rabbi Yehuda Steiger* 435.714.8590

#### S. GEORGE

*Rabbi Mendy Cohen* 862.812.6224

#### SALT LAKE CITY

*Rabbi Benny Zippel* 801.467.7777

## VERMONT

#### BURLINGTON

*Rabbi Yitzchok Raskin* 802.658.5770

#### MANCHESTER

*Rabbi Menachem Andrusier* 518.506.8678

#### WATERBURY CENTER

*Rabbi Boruch Simon* 518.360.7337

## VIRGINIA

#### ALEXANDRIA/ARLINGTON

*Rabbi Mordechai Newman* 703.370.2774

#### FAIRFAX

*Rabbi Leibel Fajnland* 703.426.1980

#### GAINESVILLE

*Rabbi Shmuel Perlstein* 571.445.0342

#### LOUDOUN COUNTY

*Rabbi Chaim Cohen* 248.298.9279

#### NORFOLK

*Rabbi Aaron Margolin*
*Rabbi Levi Brashevitzky* 757.616.0770

#### RICHMOND

*Rabbi Shlomo Pereira* 804.740.2000

#### WILLIAMSBURG

*Rabbi Mendy Heber* 234.770.0306

#### WINCHESTER

*Rabbi Yishai Dinerman* 540.324.9879

## WASHINGTON

#### BAINBRIDGE ISLAND

*Rabbi Mendy Goldshmid* 206.397.7679

#### BELLINGHAM

*Rabbi Yosef Truxton* 360.224.9919

#### ISSAQUAH

*Rabbi Schneur Matusof* 347.775.7069

#### KIRKLAND

*Rabbi Chaim S. Rivkin* 425.749.8512

#### LYNNWOOD

*Rabbi Berel Paltiel* 425.286.7465

#### MERCER ISLAND

*Rabbi Elazar Bogomilsky* 206.527.1411
*Rabbi Nissan Kornfeld* 206.851.2324

#### NORMANDY PARK

*Rabbi Moshe Wolff* 206.946.2477

#### OLYMPIA

*Rabbi Yosef Schtroks* 360.867.8804

#### SEATTLE

*Rabbi Yoni Levitin* 206.851.9831
*Rabbi Shmuel Levitin* 347.415.2271
*Rabbi Shnai Levitin* 347.342.2259
*Rabbi Yossi Rodal* 310.382.0868

#### SPOKANE COUNTY

*Rabbi Yisroel Hahn* 509.443.0770

## WISCONSIN

#### BAYSIDE

*Rabbi Cheski Edelman* 414.439.5041

#### BROOKFIELD

*Rabbi Levi Brook* 925.708.4203

#### KENOSHA

*Rabbi Tzali Wilschanski* 262.359.0770

#### MADISON

*Rabbi Avremel Matusof* 608.335.3777

#### MEQUON

*Rabbi Doobie Lisker* 323.216.6139
*Rabbi Menachem Rapoport* 262.242.2235

#### MILWAUKEE

*Rabbi Levi Emmer* 414.277.8839
*Rabbi Mendel Shmotkin* 414.961.6100

## WYOMING

#### LARAMIE

*Rabbi Yaakov Raskin* 307.920.2613

## ARGENTINA

#### BAHIA BLANCA

*Rabbi Shmuel Freedman* 347.300.2779

#### BUENOS AIRES

*Rabbi Abraham Benchimol* 54.11.6048.5333
*Rabbi Yossi Birman* 54.11.5334.6606
*Mrs. Chani Gorowitz* 54.11.4865.0445
*Rabbi Menachem M. Grunblatt* 54.911.3574.0037
*Rabbi Mendy Gurevitch* 55.11.4545.7771
*Rabbi Mendel Levy* 54.11.3687.8258
*Rabbi Shlomo Levy* 54.11.4807.2223
*Rabbi Yosef Levy* 54.11.4504.1908
*Rabbi Yosef Yitzjok Levy* 54.11.6292.4125
*Rabbi Tzvi Lipinsky* 54.11.5249.2693
*Rabbi Yossi Ludman* 54.11.3935.0214
*Rabbi Yoel Migdal* 54.11.4963.1221
*Rabbi Mendi Mizrahi* 54.11.4963.1221
*Rabbi Shiele Plotka* 54.11.4634.3111
*Rabbi Itzjak Safranchik* 54.11.3699.3977
*Rabbi Shniur Zalmen Schvetz* 54.11.3552.5208
*Rabbi Shloimi Setton* 54.11.4982.8637
*Rabbi Pinhas Sudry* 54.1.4822.2285

#### CORDOBA

*Rabbi Menajem Turk* 54.351.233.8250

#### ROSARIO

*Rabbi Shlomo Tawil* 54.93.4152.0039

#### S. MIGUEL DE TUCUMÁN

*Rabbi Ariel Levy* 54.381.473.6944

#### SALTA

*Rabbi Rafael Tawil* 54.387.421.4947

## AUSTRALIA

NEW SOUTH WALES

**BELLEVUE HILL**

*Mrs. Chaya Kaye* 614.3342.2755

**DOUBLE BAY**

*Rabbi Yanky Berger* 612.9327.1644

**DOVER HEIGHTS**

*Rabbi Motti Feldman* 614.0400.8572

**MAROUBRA**

*Rabbi Schneur Goldstein* 614.3476.0722

**NEWTOWN**

*Rabbi Eli Feldman* 614.0077.0613

**NORTH SHORE**

*Rabbi Nochum Schapiro*
*Rebbetzin Fruma Schapiro* 612.9488.9548

**SYDNEY**

*Rabbi Levi Wolff* 614.2162.2622
*Rabbi Meir Wilenkin* 614.4886.9153

**THE HILL**

*Rabbi Yossi Rodal* 614.2573.0412

QUEENSLAND

**BOKARINA**

*Rabbi Asher Goodman* 898.6763.0334

**BRISBANE**

*Rabbi Levi Jaffe* 617.3843.6770

TASMANIA

**SOUTH LAUNCESTON**

*Mrs. Rochel Gordon* 614.2055.0405

VICTORIA

**EAST S. KILDA**

*Rabbi Sholem Gorelik* 614.5244.8770

**MOORABBIN**

*Rabbi Elisha Greenbaum* 614.0349.0434

WESTERN AUSTRALIA

**PERTH**

*Rabbi Shalom White* 618.9275.2106

## AZERBAIJAN

**BAKU**

*Mrs. Chavi Segal* 994.12.597.91.90

## BELARUS

**BOBRUISK**

*Mrs. Mina Hababo* 375.29.104.3230

**MINSK**

*Rabbi Shneur Deitsch*
*Mrs. Bassie Deitsch* 375.29.330.6675

## BELGIUM

**ANTWERP**

*Rabbi Mendel Gurary* 32.48.656.9878

**BRUSSELS**

*Rabbi Shmuel Pinson* 375.29.330.6675

## BRAZIL

**CURITIBA**

*Rabbi Mendy Labkowski* 55.41.3079.1338

**S. PAULO**

*Rabbi Avraham Steinmetz* 55.11.3081.3081

## CANADA

ALBERTA

**CALGARY**

*Rabbi Mordechai Groner* 403.281.3770

**EDMONTON**

*Rabbi Ari Drelich*
*Rabbi Mendy Blachman* 780.200.5770

BRITISH COLUMBIA

**COQUITLAM**

*Rabbi Mordechai Gurevitz* 604.787.5667

**NANAIMO**

*Rabbi Benzti Shemtov* 250.797.7877

**RICHMOND**

*Rabbi Yechiel Baitelman* 604.277.6427

**VANCOUVER**

*Rabbi Dovid Rosenfeld* 604.266.1313
*Rabbi Shmuel Yeshayahu* 604.738.7060

**VICTORIA**

*Rabbi Meir Kaplan* 250.595.7656

MANITOBA

**WINNIPEG**

*Rabbi Menachem Altein* 204.869.7631
*Rabbi Shmuel Altein* 204.339.8737

ONTARIO

**BAYVIEW**

*Rabbi Levi Gansburg* 416.551.9391

**EAST THORNHILL**

*Rabbi Mendel Zaltzman* 647.998.7105

**GREATER TORONTO REGIONAL OFFICE & THORNHILL**

*Rabbi Yossi Gansburg* 905.731.7000

**INNISFIL**

*Rabbi Zevi Kaplan* 705.970.7074

**KINGSTON**

*Rabbi Yisroel Simon* 613.770.1884

**MAPLE**

*Rabbi Yechezkel Deren* 647.883.6372

**MISSISSAUGA**

*Rabbi Yitzchok Slavin* 905.820.4432

**NORTH YORK**

*Rabbi Sruli Steiner* 647.501.5618

**OTTAWA**

*Rabbi Menachem M. Blum* 613.843.7770
*Rabbi Moshe Caytak* 613.902.4394

**RICHMOND HILL**

*Rabbi Mendel Bernstein* 905.303.1880
*Rabbi Yosef Hecht* 416.837.0962

**TORONTO**

*Rabbi Menachem Gansburg* 647.409.6480
*Rabbi Shmuly Grossbaum* 648.677.0665
*Rabbi Sholom Lezell* 416.809.1365
*Rabbi Shmuel Neft* 647.966.7105
*Rabbi Moshe Steiner* 416.635.9606

WATERLOO

*Rabbi Moshe Goldman* 226.338.7770

WHITBY

*Rabbi Tzali Borenstein* 905.447.8215

WOODBRIDGE

*Rabbi Shalom Bakshi* 647.982.3419

QUEBEC

CÔTE S.-LUC

*Rabbi Levi Naparstek* 438.409.6770

DOLLARD-DES ORMEAUX

*Rabbi Leibel Fine* 514.777.4675

HAMPSTEAD

*Rabbi Moshe New*

*Rabbi Berel Bell*

*Mrs. Chanie Teitlebaum* 514.739.0770

MONTREAL

*Rabbi Ronnie Fine*

*Pesach Nussbaum* 514.738.3434

MONTREAL WEST

*Rabbi Mendy Marlow* 514.632.9649

OLD MONTREAL/GRIFFINTOWN

*Rabbi Nissan Gansbourg*

*Rabbi Berel Bell* 514.800.6966

S. LAURENT

*Rabbi Schneur Zalmen Silberstein* 514.747.1199

S. LAZARE

*Rabbi Nochum Labkowski* 514.436.7426

TOWN OF MOUNT ROYAL

*Rabbi Moshe Krasnanski*

*Rabbi Shneur Zalman Rader* 514.342.1770

SASKATCHEWAN

SASKATOON

*Rabbi Raphael Kats* 306.384.4370

## CAYMAN ISLANDS

GEORGE TOWN

*Rabbi Berel Pewzner* 717.798.1040

## COLOMBIA

BOGOTA

*Rabbi Chanoch Piekarski* 57.1.635.8251

## COSTA RICA

S. JOSÉ

*Rabbi Hershel Spalter*

*Rabbi Moshe Bitton* 506.4010.1515

## CROATIA

ZAGREB

*Rabbi Pinchas Zaklas* 385.1.481.2227

## DENMARK

COPENHAGEN

*Rabbi Yitzchok Loewenthal* 45.3316.1850

## DOMINICAN REPUBLIC

S. DOMINGO

*Rabbi Shimon Pelman* 829.341.2770

## ESTONIA

TALLINN

*Rabbi Shmuel Kot* 372.662.30.50

## FRANCE

BOULOGNE

*Rabbi Michael Sojcher* 33.1.46.99.87.85

DIJON

*Rabbi Chaim Slonim* 33.6.52.05.26.65

LA VARENNE-S.-HILAIRE

*Rabbi Mena'hem Mendel Benelbaz*
33.6.17.81.57.47

MARSEILLE

*Rabbi Eliahou Altabe* 33.6.11.60.03.05

*Rabbi Mena'hem Mendel Assouline*
33.6.64.88.25.04

*Rabbi Emmanuel Taubenblatt* 33.4.88.00.94.85

PARIS

*Rabbi Yona Hasky* 33.1.53.75.36.01

*Rabbi Acher Marciano* 33.6.15.15.01.02

*Rabbi Avraham Barou'h Pevzner*
33.6.99.64.07.70

PONTAULT-COMBAULT

*Rabbi Yossi Amar* 33.6.61.36.07.70

VILLIERS-SUR-MARNE

*Rabbi Mena'hem Mendel Mergui*
33.1.49.30.89.66

## GEORGIA

TBILISI

*Rabbi Meir Kozlovsky* 995.32.2429770

## GERMANY

BERLIN

*Rabbi Yehuda Tiechtel* 49.30.2128.0830

DUSSELDORF

*Rabbi Chaim Barkahn* 49.173.2871.770

HAMBURG

*Rabbi Shlomo Bistritzky* 49.40.4142.4190

HANNOVER 49.511.811.2822

*Chapter founded by Rabbi Binyamin Wolff, OBM*

## GREECE

ATHENS

*Rabbi Mendel Hendel* 30.210.323.3825

## GUATEMALA

GUATEMALA CITY

*Rabbi Shalom Pelman* 502.2485.0770

## HUNGARY

BUDAPEST

*Rabbi Shlomo Kovesh* 361.268.0183

## IRELAND

### DUBLIN

*Rabbi Zalman Lent* 3538.7419.5354

## ISRAEL

### ASHKELON

*Rabbi Shneor Lieberman* 054.977.0512

### BALFURYA

*Rabbi Noam Bar-Tov* 054.580.4770

### CAESAREA

*Rabbi Chaim Meir Lieberman* 054.621.2586

### EVEN YEHUDA

*Rabbi Menachem Noyman* 054.777.0707

### GANEI TIKVA

*Rabbi Gershon Shnur* 054.524.2358

### GIV'ATAYIM

*Rabbi Pinchus Bitton* 052.643.8770

### JERUSALEM

*Rabbi Levi Diamond* 055.665.7702
*Rabbi Avraham Hendel* 054.830.5799

### KARMIEL

*Rabbi Mendy Elishevitz* 054.521.3073

### KFAR SABA

*Rabbi Yossi Baitch* 054.445.5020

### KIRYAT BIALIK

*Rabbi Pinny Marton* 050.661.1768

### KIRYAT MOTZKIN

*Rabbi Shimon Eizenbach* 050.902.0770

### KOCHAV YAIR

*Rabbi Dovi Greenberg* 054.332.6244

### MACCABIM-RE'UT

*Rabbi Yosef Yitzchak Noiman* 054.977.0549

### NESS ZIONA

*Rabbi Menachem Feldman* 054.497.7092

### NETANYA

*Rabbi Schneur Brod* 054.579.7572

### RAMAT GAN-KRINITZI

*Rabbi Yisroel Gurevitz* 052.743.2814

### RAMAT GAN-MAROM NAVE

*Rabbi Binyamin Meir Kali* 050.476.0770

### RAMAT YISHAI

*Rabbi Shneor Zalman Wolosow* 052.324.5475

### RISHON LEZION

*Rabbi Uri Keshet* 050.722.4593

### ROSH PINA

*Rabbi Sholom Ber Hertzel* 052.458.7600

### TEL AVIV

*Rabbi Shneur Piekarski* 054.971.5568

## JAMAICA

### MONTEGO BAY

*Rabbi Yaakov Raskin* 876.452.3223

## JAPAN

### TOKYO

*Rabbi Mendi Sudakevich* 81.3.5789.2846

## KAZAKHSTAN

### ALMATY

*Rabbi Shevach Zlatopolsky* 7.7272.77.59.49

## KYRGYZSTAN

### BISHKEK

*Rabbi Arye Raichman* 996.312.68.19.66

## LATVIA

### RIGA

*Rabbi Shneur Zalman Kot*
*Mrs. Rivka Glazman* 371.6720.40.22

## LITHUANIA

### VILNIUS

*Rabbi Sholom Ber Krinsky* 370.6817.1367

## LUXEMBOURG

### LUXEMBOURG

*Rabbi Mendel Edelman* 352.2877.7079

## MEXICO

### PUERTO VALLARTA

*Rabbi Shneur Hecht* 52.32.2141.7279

### S. MIGUEL DE ALLENDE

*Rabbi Daniel Huebner* 52.41.5181.8092

## NETHERLANDS

### ALMERE

*Rabbi Moshe Stiefel* 31.36.744.0509

### AMSTERDAM

*Rabbi Yanki Jacobs* 31.644.988.627
*Rabbi Jaacov Zwi Spiero* 31.652.328.065

### EINDHOVEN

*Rabbi Simcha Steinberg* 31.63.635.7593

### HAGUE

*Rabbi Shmuel Katzman* 31.70.347.0222

### HEEMSTEDE-HAARLEM

*Rabbi Shmuel Spiero* 31.23.532.0707

### MAASTRICHT

*Rabbi Avrohom Cohen* 32.48.549.6766

### NIJMEGEN

*Rabbi Menachem Mendel Levine* 31.621.586.575

### ROTTERDAM

*Rabbi Yehuda Vorst* 31.10.265.5530

## PANAMA

### PANAMA CITY

*Rabbi Ari Laine*
*Rabbi Gabriel Benayon* 507.223.3383

## RUSSIA

### ASTRAKHAN

*Rabbi Yisroel Melamed* 7.851.239.28.24

#### BRYANSK

*Rabbi Menachem Mendel Zaklas* 7.483.264.55.15

#### CHELYABINSK

*Rabbi Meir Kirsh* 7.351.263.24.68

#### MOSCOW

*Rabbi Aizik Rosenfeld* 7.906.762.88.81
*Rabbi Mordechai Weisberg* 7.495.645.50.00
*Rabbi Mendel Wilansky* 7.916.572.22.41

#### NIZHNY NOVGOROD

*Rabbi Shimon Bergman* 7.920.253.47.70

#### NOVOSIBIRSK

*Rabbi Shneur Zalmen Zaklos* 7.903.900.43.22

#### OMSK

*Rabbi Osher Krichevsky* 7.381.231.33.07

#### PERM

*Rabbi Zalman Deutch* 7.342.212.47.32

#### ROSTOV

*Rabbi Chaim Danzinger* 7.8632.99.02.68

#### S. PETERSBURG

*Rabbi Shalom Pewzner* 7.911.726.21.19
*Rabbi Zvi Pinsky* 7.812.713.62.09

#### SAMARA

*Rabbi Shlomo Deutch* 7.846.333.40.64

#### SARATOV

*Rabbi Yaakov Kubitshek* 7.8452.21.58.00

#### TOGLIATTI

*Rabbi Meier Fischer* 7.848.273.02.84

#### UFA

*Rabbi Dan Krichevsky* 7.347.244.55.33

#### VORONEZH

*Rabbi Levi Stiefel* 7.473.252.96.99

### SINGAPORE

#### SINGAPORE

*Rabbi Mordechai Abergel* 656.337.2189
*Rabbi Netanel Rivni* 656.336.2127
*Classes in Hebrew*

### SOUTH AFRICA

#### JOHANNESBURG

*Rabbi Dovid Masinter*
*Rabbi Ari Kievman* 27.11.440.6600

### SWEDEN

#### STOCKHOLM

*Rabbi Chaim Greisman* 46.70.790.8994

### SWITZERLAND

#### LUZERN

*Rabbi Chaim Drukman* 41.41.361.1770

#### ZURICH

*Rabbi Mendel Rosenfeld* 41.44.289.7050

### THAILAND

#### BANGKOK

*Rabbi Yosef C. Kantor* 6681.837.7618

### UKRAINE

#### BERDITCHEV

*Mrs. Chana Thaler* 380.637.70.37.70

#### DNEPROPETROVSK

*Rabbi Dan Makagon* 380.504.51.13.18

#### NIKOLAYEV

*Rabbi Sholom Gotlieb* 380.512.37.37.71

#### ODESSA

*Rabbi Avraham Wolf*
*Rabbi Yaakov Neiman* 38.048.728.0770 EXT. 280

#### ZAPOROZHYE

*Mrs. Nechama Dina Ehrentreu* 380.957.19.96.08

#### ZHITOMIR

*Rabbi Shlomo Wilhelm* 380.504.63.01.32

### UNITED KINGDOM

#### ALTRINCHAM

*Rabbi Mendel Chein* 44.793.589.5600

#### BOURNEMOUTH

*Rabbi Bentzion Alperowitz* 44.749.456.7177

#### CHEADLE

*Rabbi Peretz Chein* 44.161.428.1818

ESSEX

#### EPPING

*Rabbi Yossi Posen* 44.749.650.4345

#### LEEDS

*Rabbi Eli Pink* 44.113.266.3311

#### LONDON

*Rabbi Moshe Adler* 44.771.052.4460
*Rabbi Boruch Altein* 44.749.612.3342
*Rabbi Mendel Cohen* 44.736.640.8244
*Rabbi Mechel Gancz* 44.758.332.3074
*Rabbi Chaim Hoch* 44.753.879.9524
*Rabbi Mendel Kalmenson* 44.758.592.0195
*Rabbi Dovid Katz* 44.207.625.2682
*Mrs. Esther Kesselman* 44.794.432.4829
*Rabbi Mendy Korer* 44.794.632.5444
*Rabbi Baruch Levin* 44.208.905.4141
*Rabbi Eli Levin* 44.754.046.1568
*Rabbi Yisroel Lew* 44.787.987.1571
*Mrs. Chanie Simon* 44.208.458.0416
*Rabbi Bentzi Sudak* 44.781.211.1890
*Rabbi Yisroel Weisz* 44.797.652.2807
*Rabbi Shneur Wineberg* 44.745.628.6538

#### MANCHESTER

*Rabbi Levi Cohen* 44.161.792.6335
*Rabbi Shmuli Jaffe* 44.161.766.1812

#### NOTTINGHAM

*Rabbi Mendy Lent* 44.759.005.1261

#### RADLETT, HERTFORDSHIRE

*Rabbi Alexander Sender Dubrawsky* 44.794.380.8965

# The Jewish Learning Multiplex

*Brought to you by the Rohr Jewish Learning Institute*

In fulfillment of the mandate of the Lubavitcher Rebbe, of blessed memory, whose leadership guides every step of our work, the mission of the Rohr Jewish Learning Institute is to transform Jewish life and the greater community through the study of Torah, connecting each Jew to our shared heritage of Jewish learning.

While our flagship program remains the cornerstone of our organization, JLI is proud to feature additional divisions catering to specific populations, in order to meet a wide array of educational needs.

*The Rohr*
**JEWISH LEARNING INSTITUTE**

A subsidiary of Merkos L'Inyonei Chinuch, the adult education arm of the Chabad-Lubavitch movement

Torah Studies provides a rich and nuanced encounter with the weekly Torah reading.

Jewish teens forge their identity as they engage in Torah study, social interaction, and serious fun.

The Rosh Chodesh Society gathers Jewish women together once a month for intensive textual study.

SHABBAT
in the HEIGHTS

A spirited Shabbos experience, rich in Jewish learning, connection, and unity, in the Chabad movement's beating heart.

LAND & SPIRIT

Participants delve into our nation's past while exploring the Holy Land's relevance and meaning today.

NATIONAL JEWISH RETREAT

This yearly event rejuvenates mind, body, and spirit with a powerful synthesis of Jewish learning and community.

THE
LIVING JEWISH
SERIES

A comprehensive series of courses guiding Jews through every aspect of practical observant life and its meaning.

Addressing life's biggest questions to help high school students unlock joy and meaning in Torah and *mitzvot.*

MyShiur courses are designed to assist students in developing the skills needed to study Talmud independently.

Select affiliates are invited to partner with peers and noted professionals, as leaders of innovation and excellence.

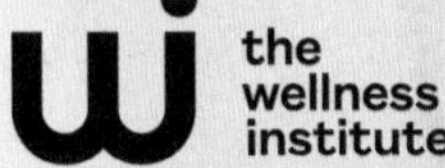


Equips youths facing adulthood with education and resources to address youth mental health

This rigorous fellowship program invites select college students to explore the fundamentals of Judaism.

TorahCafe.com provides an exclusive selection of top-rated Jewish educational videos.

Machon Shmuel is an institute providing Torah research in the service of educators worldwide.

A prestigious program that awards recognition and academic credentials to high school students who complete JLI Teens' comprehensive course of Jewish study.

Empowering Jews worldwide with knowledge and confidence to embrace a deep connection to Israel as acore aspect of Jewish identity.

Thought-provoking and engaging curricula on foundational aspects of Torah and Chasidus designed for use in Chabad yeshivos.

Read it in Hebrew is a crash course that teaches adults to read Hebrew in just five sessions.

# JLI GETAWAYS

*Experience the Land.*
*Discover its soul.*

**LANDANDSPIRIT.ORG**

*Experience Shabbat in*
*Chabad's spiritual hometown.*

**SHABBATINTHEHEIGHTS.COM**

*Elevate your mind.*
*Embrace connection.*
*Cultivate community.*

**JRETREAT.COM**